SHAH MOHAMMED

Strategy Ikigai

28 Key Business Strategy Principles from the World's Top Companies

Copyright © 2024 by Shah Mohammed

All rights reserved. No part of this publication may be reproduced, stored or transmitted in any form or by any means, electronic, mechanical, photocopying, recording, scanning, or otherwise without written permission from the publisher. It is illegal to copy this book, post it to a website, or distribute it by any other means without permission.

First edition

This book was professionally typeset on Reedsy.
Find out more at reedsy.com

Contents

Introduction v

1. The Principle of Vision — 1
2. The Principle of Core Values — 6
3. The Principle of Customer Centricity — 12
4. The Principle of Hiring Right People — 19
5. The Principle of Value Proposition — 23
6. The Principle of Customer Segments — 29
7. The Principle of Focus — 36
8. The Principle of Differentiation — 43
9. The Principle of Core Competencies — 49
10. The Principle of Strategic Activities — 52
11. The Principle of Tradeoffs — 61
12. The Principle of Strategic Fit — 66
13. The Principle of Key Resources — 72
14. The Principle of Key Partners — 78
15. The Principle of Customer Relationships — 81
16. The Principle of Communication Channels — 86
17. The Principle of Big Picture — 92
18. The Principle of Attention to Detail (Thinking Small) — 98
19. The Principle of Financial Management — 105
20. The Principle of Cost Structure — 109
21. The Principle of Revenue Streams — 115
22. The Principle of Culture — 121
23. The Principle of Branding — 126
24. The Principle of Rapid Prototyping, Testing, and Iteration — 130
25. The Principle of Execution — 134

26	The Principle of Storytelling	138
27	The Principle of Anticipating Trends	146
28	The Principle of Winning Attitude	150
29	Putting It All Together - Implementing Your Business...	155
About the Author		159
Also by Shah Mohammed		161

Introduction

In the ever-evolving world of business, crafting a winning strategy is essential for long-term success. A well-designed strategy serves as a roadmap, guiding an organization towards its desired future state while effectively navigating the challenges and opportunities that arise along the way.

However, developing a robust and effective business strategy is no simple task. It requires a deep understanding of various fundamental principles that underpin the very essence of strategic thinking and decision-making. These principles, when applied in harmony, create a solid foundation upon which a business can build, grow, and thrive.

In this book, we will embark on a journey to explore the key principles that lie at the heart of building a successful business strategy. Each chapter will dive into a specific principle, providing insights, case studies, and practical tools to help you understand and apply these concepts within your own organization.

From defining a clear vision and core values to understanding your customers and crafting a compelling value proposition, we will cover the essential building blocks of strategy formulation. We will delve into the importance of focus, differentiation, and leveraging your core competencies to establish a competitive edge in the market.

The principles of strategic activities, tradeoffs, and strategic fit will be examined, highlighting the critical role they play in creating a cohesive and effective strategy. We will also explore the significance of key resources, partnerships, and customer relationships in executing your strategy and driving growth.

Throughout the book, we will emphasize the importance of maintaining a big-picture perspective while paying attention to the finer details that can make or break your strategy. Financial management, organizational culture, and the art of hiring the right people will be discussed as crucial elements in bringing your strategy to life.

We will also touch upon the power of branding, the value of rapid prototyping and iteration, and the need to carefully manage your cost structure and revenue streams. The principles of execution, storytelling, anticipating trends, and cultivating a winning attitude will be highlighted as key drivers of strategic success.

By the end of this book, you will have gained a comprehensive understanding of the fundamental principles that shape a winning business strategy. You will be equipped with the knowledge to analyze your current strategy, identify areas for improvement, and develop a roadmap for future growth and success.

Whether you are an entrepreneur, a business leader, or a student of strategy, this book will provide you with a solid foundation upon which to build your strategic thinking skills. So, let us embark on this journey together, unlocking the secrets to building a successful business strategy, one principle at a time.

* * *

1

The Principle of Vision

In business strategy, few elements hold as much power and potential as a clear and compelling vision. A well-crafted vision serves as the guiding light for an organization, illuminating the path to long-term success and providing a foundation upon which all strategic decisions are built. It is the north star that keeps a company focused, motivated, and aligned in the face of challenges and opportunities alike.

At its core, a vision is a vivid, aspirational description of what an organization aims to achieve in the future. It goes beyond mere goals or objectives, painting a picture of the ideal state the company seeks to create. A strong vision statement is not just a bland, generic phrase; it is a living, breathing embodiment of the company's purpose, values, and desired impact on the world.

Effective vision statements share several key characteristics. They are aspirational, stretching the organization beyond its current capabilities and daring to imagine a better future. They are future-oriented, looking beyond the constraints of the present to envision what could be. They are clear and concise, easily understood and remembered by all stakeholders. And they are memorable, leaving a lasting impression that inspires and motivates action.

Take, for example, the vision statement of Microsoft: "To empower every person and every organization on the planet to achieve more." This simple yet powerful phrase encapsulates the company's purpose, values, and desired impact in just a few words. It is aspirational, future-oriented, clear, concise, and memorable – all the hallmarks of a strong vision.

The benefits of having a strong vision are manifold. First and foremost, it provides direction and purpose for the organization. When everyone from the CEO to the front-line employees understands and buys into the vision, they are more likely to make decisions and take actions that align with that vision. This alignment is crucial for long-term success, as it ensures that all efforts are focused on achieving the same overarching goal.

A compelling vision also inspires and motivates employees. When people feel connected to a higher purpose and believe in the future the company is working towards, they are more engaged, productive, and committed to their work. This sense of meaning and purpose can be a powerful driver of employee satisfaction, retention, and performance.

Moreover, a strong vision guides decision-making and resource allocation. When faced with difficult choices or competing priorities, leaders can ask themselves, "Which option best aligns with and supports our vision?" This clarity of purpose streamlines decision-making and ensures that resources are invested in initiatives that move the company closer to its desired future state.

A compelling vision also attracts customers, partners, and investors who share the company's values and aspirations. When external stakeholders understand and believe in the vision, they are more likely to choose to do business with, partner with, or invest in the company. This alignment of values and purpose can lead to stronger, more fruitful relationships and a broader base of support for the organization.

Perhaps most importantly, a strong vision sets the foundation for long-term success and legacy. It defines the ultimate aim and impact the company seeks to achieve, not just in the next quarter or year, but over the course of its existence. By keeping this long-term perspective in mind, leaders can make decisions and investments that may not pay off immediately but will ultimately lead to greater success and impact down the road.

So, how can a company go about crafting its own powerful vision? The process begins with a deep understanding of the company's purpose and values. Leaders must ask themselves, "Why do we exist? What do we stand for? What impact do we want to have on the world?" The answers to these questions form the bedrock upon which the vision is built.

Next, leaders must envision the future they want to create. This involves looking beyond the constraints and challenges of the present to imagine what could be possible if the company were to fully live out its purpose and values. What would the world look like if the company achieved its full potential? What would be different? What would be better?

Involving key stakeholders in the visioning process is also crucial. Gathering input and perspectives from employees, customers, partners, and other stakeholders helps ensure that the vision is inclusive, relevant, and resonant. It also helps build buy-in and commitment to the vision from the outset.

Once the vision has been crafted, it must be refined and communicated effectively. This involves distilling the vision down to its essence, ensuring that it is clear, concise, and memorable. It also involves sharing the vision widely and consistently, embedding it into all aspects of the company's communication and culture.

But crafting a strong vision is only the beginning. To truly harness the power of vision, companies must align their strategy and actions with that vision. This involves translating the vision into concrete goals, objectives, and initiatives. It means ensuring that all decisions and actions, from the boardroom to the front lines, support and further the vision. And it requires regularly reviewing and adjusting the strategy to ensure that it remains true to the vision, even as the business environment changes.

Leading with vision is also paramount. Leaders must champion and embody the vision, living it out in their own actions and decisions. They must inspire others to buy into and contribute to the vision, painting a compelling picture of the future and enlisting their support and engagement. And they must be willing to stay the course and hold true to the vision, even in the face of challenges, setbacks, and short-term pressures.

There are countless examples of companies that have harnessed the power of vision to achieve remarkable success. Take Apple, whose vision of "creating products that people love" has guided the company's innovation and design for decades. Or Patagonia, whose vision of "using business to inspire and implement solutions to the environmental crisis" has made it a leader in sustainable business practices.

These companies, and many others like them, demonstrate the transformative power of a strong, compelling vision. They show that when a company knows where it wants to go and why, and when it aligns its strategy, actions, and leadership with that vision, it can achieve extraordinary things.

In conclusion, the Principle of Vision is a crucial foundation for successful business strategy. A clear, compelling vision provides direction, inspiration, and alignment for an organization, guiding it towards long-term success and impact.

Tesla

Tesla's vision statement is "to accelerate the world's transition to sustainable energy." This simple yet powerful phrase encapsulates the company's purpose, values, and desired impact on a global scale. It's a vision that goes beyond just selling electric cars; it's about transforming the entire transportation and energy industries to create a more sustainable future for all.

Under the leadership of CEO Elon Musk, Tesla has consistently aligned its strategy and actions with this vision. From developing increasingly affordable and efficient electric vehicles to investing in renewable energy solutions like solar panels and battery storage, every aspect of Tesla's business is focused on advancing its vision of a sustainable energy future.

This unwavering commitment to its vision has helped Tesla overcome numerous challenges and setbacks, from production delays to skepticism from industry incumbents. It has also inspired a passionate and loyal customer base, who view Tesla not just as a car company, but as a movement towards a better future.

Tesla's impact is already being felt around the world. The company has accelerated the adoption of electric vehicles, forcing traditional automakers to invest heavily in EV development. It has also pushed the boundaries of battery technology, driving down costs and improving efficiency to make renewable energy more viable and accessible.

TED

TED (Technology, Entertainment, Design) is a nonprofit organization whose vision is "to spread ideas." Since its founding in 1984, TED has been dedicated to the belief that ideas have the power to change the world, and that by sharing those ideas widely, it can create positive impact on a global scale.

TED's vision comes to life through its signature TED Talks, short, powerful speeches given by experts and thought leaders on a wide range of topics. By carefully curating and sharing these talks online for free, TED has made knowledge and inspiration accessible to millions of people around the world.

The organization's commitment to its vision extends beyond just the talks themselves. TED also hosts conferences, awards grants to innovative ideas, and supports educational initiatives to empower the next generation of changemakers. Every aspect of TED's operations is designed to further its mission of spreading ideas and sparking positive change.

TED's impact has been profound. Its talks have been viewed billions of times, inspiring countless people to take action on issues ranging from climate change to social justice. The organization has also helped elevate important ideas and voices that might have otherwise gone unheard, giving a platform to a diverse range of perspectives and experiences.

Perhaps most importantly, TED has helped create a global community united by a shared belief in the power of ideas. By bringing together people from all walks of life to listen, learn, and be inspired, TED has fostered a sense of connection and possibility that transcends borders and boundaries.

* * *

2

The Principle of Core Values

Core values are the bedrock of any successful organization, serving as the unwavering principles that guide decision-making, shape culture, and define a company's character. These deeply held beliefs are more than mere words; they are the very essence of a company's identity and purpose.

At their essence, core values are the fundamental, enduring tenets that define a company's character and guide its behavior. They are the non-negotiable principles that shape how the organization operates, how its people interact, and how it engages with the world around it. Core values are not merely aspirational statements or temporary fads; they are the bedrock upon which the company's very identity is built.

Consider some examples of core values from successful companies. Zappos, the online shoe retailer, has "Deliver WOW Through Service" as one of its core values, reflecting its commitment to exceptional customer experiences. Patagonia, the outdoor apparel company, has "Use Business to Protect Nature" as a core value, guiding its decisions around sustainability and environmental responsibility. Google's core values include "Focus on the user and all else will follow," highlighting its user-centric approach to innovation.

The benefits of having strong, clearly articulated core values are significant. First and foremost, core values create a shared sense of identity and purpose among employees. When everyone in the organization understands and embraces the same guiding principles, it fosters a sense of unity and belonging. People feel connected to something larger than themselves and are motivated to contribute to the company's mission.

Core values also serve as a framework for decision-making at all levels of the organization. When faced with difficult choices or competing priorities, employees can ask themselves, "Which option best aligns with our core values?" This clarity and consistency in decision-making helps ensure that the company stays true to its purpose and avoids ethical or reputational pitfalls.

Strong core values also play a crucial role in attracting and retaining employees who are a good fit for the company's culture. When a company's values are clearly communicated and consistently lived out, it attracts people who share those same beliefs and principles. This alignment of values leads to higher levels of employee engagement, productivity, and retention, as people feel a deep sense of connection and commitment to the organization.

Beyond the internal benefits, strong core values also build trust and loyalty with customers and external stakeholders. When a company consistently acts in accordance with its stated values, it demonstrates integrity and authenticity. Customers come to trust that the company will do what it says and stand behind its products or services. This trust translates into brand loyalty, advocacy, and long-term business success.

So, how can a company go about identifying and developing its core values? The process begins with deep reflection on the company's history, culture, and purpose. Leaders must ask themselves, "What beliefs and principles have guided us from the start? What do we stand for? What would we never compromise on?"

Involving employees and stakeholders in this process is also crucial. Seeking input and perspectives from people across the organization helps ensure that the articulated values resonate and reflect the lived experience of the company. It also helps build buy-in and ownership of the values from the outset.

As the core values take shape, it's important to distinguish them from aspirational or permission-to-play values. True core values should be authentic, enduring, and non-negotiable. They should also be specific and actionable, providing clear guidance for behavior and decision-making. Refining and articulating the core values in a clear, concise way is key to ensuring they are easily understood and remembered by all.

Once the core values have been identified, the real work begins: integrating them into every aspect of the business strategy and operations. This involves aligning goals, decisions, and actions with the core values at every level of the organization. It means incorporating the values into hiring, onboarding, and performance management processes to ensure that everyone in the company is held accountable to living out the values.

Reinforcing the core values through consistent communication, recognition, and rewards is also essential. Leaders must regularly highlight examples of the values in action, celebrate those who exemplify them, and provide opportunities for employees to discuss and apply the values in their work. When behaviors or decisions arise that conflict with the core values, it's crucial to address them promptly and consistently, reaffirming the importance of the values.

Leading and living the core values starts at the top. Leaders must embody and champion the values in their own actions and decisions, setting the tone for the rest of the organization. They must also create a culture where the values are consistently reinforced and upheld, even in the face of challenges or pressures to compromise.

Empowering employees to apply the core values in their work is also key. When people at all levels of the organization feel ownership and responsibility for living out the values, it creates a self-reinforcing culture of integrity and purpose. Regular assessment and reflection on how well the organization is aligning with its values is also important, as it allows for continuous improvement and course correction.

There are many real-world examples of companies that have successfully leveraged the power of core values to drive long-term success. Whole Foods Market, for instance, has a set of core values that include "Selling the Highest Quality Natural and Organic Products Available" and "Supporting Team Member Happiness and Excellence." These values guide everything from the products the company sells to the way it treats its employees, resulting in a strong brand reputation and loyal customer base.

Another example is Atlassian, the software company behind products like Jira and Trello. Atlassian's core values include "Open Company, No Bullshit" and "Don't #@!% the Customer." These values reflect a commitment to transparency, honesty, and customer centricity that has helped the company build trust and thrive in a competitive industry.

Of course, implementing and living out core values is not without its challenges. One common pitfall is developing values that are too generic or aspirational, lacking the specificity and authenticity needed to truly guide behavior. Another challenge is ensuring that the values are consistently lived out across the organization, rather than just being words on a wall.

Overcoming resistance or cynicism towards core values is also a common hurdle. Some employees may view the values as mere window dressing or may struggle to see how they apply to their day-to-day work. Leaders must be proactive in addressing these concerns, providing clear examples and expectations, and creating opportunities for dialogue and feedback.

Balancing core values with other business priorities and pressures can also be a challenge. In the face of short-term demands or competing interests, it can be tempting to compromise on the values. However, it's in these moments that the true test of a company's commitment to its values lies. By staying true to its core even in difficult times, a company builds resilience, trust, and long-term success.

In conclusion, the Principle of Core Values is a vital component of successful business strategy. By identifying, articulating, and living out a set of authentic, enduring principles, companies can create a strong foundation for culture, decision-making, and long-term success.

Examples—Brands and its Core Values

01 Hubspot

- Think Long Term and Solve For The Customer
- Commit Maniacally to both Mission and metrics
- Be Remarkably Transparent
- Have Empathy
- Favour Autonomy. and Take Ownership
- Be Amazing, Be Humble

02 Hootsuite

- Lead with Humility
- Strengthen the Team
- Actively Create What's Next
- Passionately Serve Customers
- Grit In All We Do
- Fiercely Champion Diversity, Equity & Inclusion

03 Nordstrom

- Customer Obsessed
- Owners at Heart
- Curious and Ever Changing
- Here to Win
- We Extend Ourselves

04 Dell

- Customer
- Integrity
- Winning Together
- Innovation
- Results

05 Percolate

- Put Customers First
- Be Respectful
- Work Fearlessly
- Think Creatively
- Stay Positive

06 Etsy

- We are a mindful, transparent, and humane business
- We plan and build for the long term
- We value craftsmanship in all we make
- We believe fun should be part of everything we do
- We keep it real, always

* * *

3

The Principle of Customer Centricity

In the world of business, success is not just about having a great product or service; it's about understanding and catering to the needs of your customers. This is where the principle of customer centricity comes into play.

At its core, customer centricity is about recognizing that a business exists because of its customers. Without customers, there would be no revenue, no growth, and no reason for the business to operate. Therefore, it is essential to understand that the customer is the most critical aspect of any business, and their needs, desires, and pain points should be the driving force behind every strategic decision.

Understanding customer needs is the first step towards achieving customer centricity. This involves conducting thorough market research, analyzing customer data, and engaging with customers directly to gain insights into their preferences, behaviors, and expectations. By understanding what customers want and need, businesses can tailor their products, services, and experiences to meet those needs effectively.

One of the most important aspects of customer centricity is empathy. Businesses must put themselves in their customers' shoes and view everything from their perspective. This means considering how customers interact with the brand, what challenges they face, and what experiences they desire. By empathizing with customers, businesses can create solutions that address their pain points and exceed their expectations.

Another critical component of customer centricity is communication. Businesses must establish open and transparent communication channels with their customers to build trust and foster long-lasting relationships. This involves actively listening to customer feedback, addressing their concerns promptly, and keeping them informed about new products, services, or changes that may affect them.

Customer centricity also plays a crucial role in shaping a company's value proposition. A value proposition is a promise of value that a business delivers to its customers, and it should be based on a deep understanding of customer needs and preferences. By crafting a compelling value proposition that resonates with customers, businesses can differentiate themselves from competitors and establish a strong brand identity.

Moreover, customer centricity should influence every aspect of a business's operations, from product development and marketing to sales and customer support. Every department and employee should be aligned around the goal of creating exceptional customer experiences and delivering value at every touchpoint.

For example, when designing new products or features, businesses should involve customers in the process through focus groups, surveys, or beta testing. This allows them to gather valuable feedback and insights that can inform product improvements and ensure that the final offering meets customer needs effectively.

Similarly, when developing marketing campaigns, businesses should focus on creating content and messages that resonate with their target audience. This involves understanding their customers' preferences, interests, and communication styles and tailoring the messaging accordingly. By speaking directly to customers in a way that they appreciate and understand, businesses can build stronger connections and drive engagement.

In the field of customer support, businesses must prioritize responsiveness, empathy, and problem-solving. When customers reach out for assistance, they expect to be heard, understood, and supported in a timely and effective manner. By investing in robust customer support systems and training employees to handle customer inquiries with care and professionalism, businesses can turn potentially negative experiences into opportunities to build loyalty and advocacy.

Ultimately, customer centricity is about creating a culture that puts the customer first in every decision and interaction. This requires a shift in mindset from a product-centric or sales-centric approach to a customer-centric one. It involves empowering employees to think like customers, providing them with the tools and resources they need to deliver exceptional experiences, and recognizing and rewarding customer-centric behaviors.

To successfully implement customer centricity, businesses must also embrace data and technology. By leveraging customer data and analytics, businesses can gain valuable insights into customer behavior, preferences, and trends. This information can then be used to personalize experiences, anticipate needs, and make data-driven decisions that enhance customer satisfaction and loyalty.

Furthermore, technology can play a significant role in enabling customer centricity. From customer relationship management (CRM) systems that help businesses manage customer interactions and data to chatbots and self-service portals that provide 24/7 support, technology can help businesses scale their customer-centric efforts and deliver seamless experiences across channels.

However, it's important to recognize that customer centricity is not a one-time initiative but an ongoing commitment. Customer needs and expectations are constantly evolving, and businesses must be agile and adaptable to stay ahead of the curve. This requires a culture of continuous learning, experimentation, and improvement, where customer feedback is actively sought and used to drive innovation and growth.

In conclusion, the principle of customer centricity is the backbone of successful businesses in today's competitive landscape. By putting the customer at the center of every decision and interaction, businesses can create products, services, and experiences that resonate with their target audience, build lasting relationships, and drive sustainable growth.

Amazon

Amazon's mission statement, "to be Earth's most customer-centric company," clearly demonstrates its commitment to putting the customer first in every aspect of its business. From its humble beginnings as an online bookstore, Amazon has consistently focused on understanding and meeting customer needs, which has been instrumental in its growth and success.

One of the key ways Amazon puts customer centricity into practice is through its obsession with customer feedback. The company actively seeks and analyzes customer reviews, ratings, and comments to gain insights into customer preferences, pain points, and expectations. This feedback is used to inform product development, improve service quality, and enhance the overall customer experience.

For example, Amazon's product recommendations are based on a deep understanding of customer behavior and preferences. By analyzing purchase history, browsing behavior, and other data points, Amazon can make personalized recommendations that help customers discover new products they may like, thus increasing customer satisfaction and loyalty.

Another way Amazon demonstrates customer centricity is through its commitment to convenience and fast delivery. The company has invested heavily in its logistics and fulfillment infrastructure to ensure that customers can receive their orders quickly and reliably. From same-day delivery to the introduction of Amazon Prime, which offers free and fast shipping among other benefits, Amazon has consistently pushed the boundaries of what's possible to make the shopping experience as seamless and convenient as possible for customers.

Amazon's customer-centric approach also extends to its customer service. The company offers multiple channels for customers to seek assistance, including phone, email, and live chat support. Amazon's customer service representatives are trained to prioritize customer needs, respond promptly and empathetically, and go above and beyond to resolve issues and ensure customer satisfaction.

In addition, Amazon has implemented various self-service options, such as detailed product information, FAQs, and customer reviews, which empower customers to make informed decisions and find answers to their questions without needing to contact customer support.

Innovation is another area where Amazon's customer centricity shines. The company is known for its willingness to experiment and take risks to create new products and services that meet evolving customer needs. From the launch of Amazon Prime Video and Amazon Music to the introduction of voice-controlled devices like Alexa, Amazon has consistently pushed the boundaries of what's possible to deliver value to customers in new and innovative ways.

Furthermore, Amazon's customer-centric culture is deeply ingrained in its leadership principles. The company's 14 leadership principles, which guide decision-making and behavior at all levels of the organization, place a strong emphasis on customer obsession, ownership, and long-term thinking. By aligning its culture and values around customer centricity, Amazon has created a shared sense of purpose and accountability that drives its success.

In summary, Amazon's example illustrates the power of customer centricity as a guiding principle for business strategy. By placing the customer at the heart of every decision, investing in innovation and convenience, and fostering a culture of customer obsession, Amazon has set a high bar for what it means to be a customer-centric company.

Gaining Customer Insights

To truly put customer centricity into practice, businesses must have a deep understanding of their customers. This requires a systematic approach to gathering, analyzing, and acting on customer insights. Here are some key methods for gaining customer insights:

1. **Customer feedback:** Actively seeking and listening to customer feedback is one of the most direct ways to gain insights. This can be done through surveys, customer reviews, social media monitoring, and direct conversations with customers. Encourage customers to share their

opinions, experiences, and suggestions, and make it easy for them to do so through various channels.
2. **Customer data analysis:** Businesses today have access to vast amounts of customer data, from purchase history and website behavior to demographic information and social media activity. By analyzing this data, businesses can identify patterns, preferences, and trends that can inform product development, marketing strategies, and customer service improvements.
3. **Customer journey mapping:** Creating a visual representation of the customer journey, from initial awareness to post-purchase experience, can help businesses identify pain points, opportunities for improvement, and moments of truth where customer loyalty is won or lost. By understanding the customer journey, businesses can design experiences that meet customer needs at every touchpoint.
4. **Ethnographic research:** Observing customers in their natural environment, such as through in-home visits or shop-alongs, can provide valuable insights into how customers use products, navigate challenges, and make decisions. This type of immersive research can uncover unmet needs and inspire new product or service ideas.
5. **Voice of the Customer (VoC) programs:** Implementing a formal VoC program can help businesses systematically gather, analyze, and act on customer feedback. This involves collecting customer data from multiple sources, using text analytics and sentiment analysis to identify key themes and emotions, and closing the loop with customers by communicating how their feedback was used to drive improvements.
6. **A/B testing:** Conducting A/B tests, where different versions of a product, website, or marketing campaign are tested with different customer segments, can help businesses optimize the customer experience based on real-world behavior. By comparing how customers respond to different variations, businesses can make data-driven decisions that improve customer satisfaction and conversions.
7. **Customer co-creation:** Involving customers in the product development process, through focus groups, beta testing, or crowdsourcing, can

help businesses create offerings that truly meet customer needs. By collaborating with customers and incorporating their insights and ideas, businesses can create a sense of shared ownership and loyalty.

To effectively turn customer insights into action, businesses need to have the right technology, processes, and culture in place. This includes investing in customer relationship management (CRM) systems, data analytics tools, and customer feedback platforms, as well as fostering a culture of curiosity, experimentation, and continuous improvement.

It's also important to ensure that customer insights are shared and acted upon across the organization, from the C-suite to the front lines. This requires breaking down silos, establishing cross-functional teams, and empowering employees to make customer-centric decisions based on data and insights.

By prioritizing customer insights and using them to inform every aspect of the business, companies can create a virtuous cycle of customer centricity. The more businesses understand and meet customer needs, the more loyal and engaged customers become, leading to greater insights and opportunities for innovation and growth. In today's customer-driven world, the ability to gain and act on customer insights is not just a nice-to-have but a critical competitive advantage.

* * *

4

The Principle of Hiring Right People

The Principle of Hiring Right People is a fundamental tenet of building a successful business strategy. It recognizes that the success of an organization is not just about the products or services it offers, but about the people who create, deliver, and support them. From the visionary leaders at the helm to the front-line employees interacting with customers, the quality and fit of the people within an organization can make or break its strategic ambitions.

The transformative power of hiring the right people is exemplified by the story of David Maxwell, who became the CEO of the struggling company, Fannie Mae, in 1981. Faced with the daunting task of turning around the organization's fortunes, Maxwell's first step was to focus on getting the right people on the Fannie Mae management team. He understood that without the right talent in place, any strategic initiatives would be doomed to fail. By prioritizing the recruitment and retention of high-quality individuals who shared the company's vision and values, Maxwell laid the foundation for Fannie Mae's subsequent success.

Similarly, when Kimberly-Clark made the strategic decision to sell its mills and exit the paper business, CEO Darwin Smith made it clear that the company would retain its best people, even though they had little or no consumer experience. Smith recognized that the knowledge, skills, and dedication of these individuals were valuable assets that could be applied to the company's new strategic direction. By keeping the right people on board and investing in their development, Kimberly-Clark was able to successfully navigate a major strategic shift and emerge stronger on the other side.

The importance of hiring the right people is further underscored by the words of Walter Bruckart, Vice President of Circuit City, who attributed the company's transition from mediocrity to excellence to its disciplined approach to talent acquisition. Bruckart emphasized that the key factors driving the company's success were all related to people – from the quality of the individuals hired to the way they were developed and empowered to contribute to the organization's goals. This focus on hiring the right people allowed Circuit City to build a strong, capable team that could execute its strategic vision with skill and dedication.

The idea that hiring smart people and then trusting them to guide the organization's direction is a powerful one, and it is echoed by visionary leaders like Steve Jobs. Jobs famously said, "It doesn't make sense to hire smart people and then tell them what to do; We hire smart people so that they can tell us what to do." This philosophy recognizes that the best strategic insights and innovations often come from the talented individuals within an organization, rather than being dictated from the top down. By hiring the right people and giving them the autonomy to shape the company's direction, leaders can tap into a wealth of knowledge, creativity, and problem-solving ability that can drive the organization forward.

The success of Netflix, one of the most disruptive and innovative companies of the modern era, can be largely attributed to its focus on hiring the right people from the very beginning. Founders Marc Randolph and Reed Hastings made a conscious effort to hire individuals who shared their dream of building a consumer-oriented company, who were passionate about their work, and who enjoyed solving user problems. They drew heavily from their own networks to find early recruits who had the skills, experience, and mindset to help bring their vision to life.

One of the key areas where Netflix's hiring strategy paid off was in its focus on bringing in people with a deep understanding of consumer behavior in the field of movies. Early hires like Mitch Lowe, who had spent thousands of hours observing consumers and running a rental chain, brought valuable insights into what people wanted from a movie rental service. Eric Meyer, the designer of the first Netflix website, was passionate about creating a user-friendly interface that would make it easy for customers to find and rent the movies they loved. And Ted Sarandos, who would go on to become Netflix's chief content officer and help turn the company into an entertainment powerhouse, brought a wealth of knowledge about movies and the entertainment industry, despite being a college dropout who had worked in video stores for years.

This focus on hiring people with the right skills, experience, and passion for the business has remained a key part of Netflix's culture as the company has grown and evolved. Managers at Netflix are deeply involved in every step of the hiring process, constantly asking themselves whether they have the right team in place to achieve their strategic goals. They recognize that having the right people on board is not a one-time event, but an ongoing process of evaluation and adjustment to ensure that the organization has the talent it needs to succeed.

The Principle of Hiring Right People is not just about finding individuals with the right skills and experience, but also about ensuring that they fit with the organization's culture and values. A company's culture is the glue that holds it together, the shared beliefs, behaviors, and norms that shape how people work together and how they approach challenges and opportunities. When new hires are a good fit with the company's culture, they are more likely to thrive and contribute to the organization's success. Conversely, when there is a mismatch between an individual's values and those of the organization, it can lead to friction, disengagement, and ultimately, underperformance.

To ensure that new hires are a good cultural fit, many companies have developed robust interview processes that go beyond assessing technical skills and experience. They may ask behavioral questions that probe candidates' attitudes, motivations, and approach to work, or use personality assessments to gain insights into their communication styles, decision-making processes, and teamwork abilities. Some companies even involve current employees in the hiring process, recognizing that they are often the best judges of whether a candidate will fit in with the existing team and contribute to a positive work environment.

Once the right people are on board, the focus shifts to retaining them and helping them grow and develop within the organization. This is where the Principle of Hiring Right People intersects with other key principles of building a successful business strategy, such as the Principle of Culture and the Principle of Focus. By creating a strong, positive culture that values learning, innovation, and collaboration, companies can create an environment where talented individuals want to stay and contribute their best work. And by providing opportunities for growth, development, and advancement, they can help their best people reach their full potential and take on increasingly important roles within the organization.

Ultimately, the Principle of Hiring Right People is about recognizing that a company's most valuable asset is its people. By investing time, resources, and attention into finding, developing, and retaining the right talent, organizations can create a powerful strategic advantage that is difficult for competitors to replicate. As Jim Collins notes in his book "Good to Great," the best companies are those that "first got the right people on the bus, the wrong people off the bus, and the right people in the right seats – and then they figured out where to drive it." By putting people first and building a strong, capable team, companies can set themselves up for long-term success and achieve their most ambitious strategic goals.

* * *

5

The Principle of Value Proposition

A strong value proposition is the foundation upon which a business builds its strategy, guiding decisions about product development, marketing, and customer engagement.

But what exactly is a value proposition? In essence, it is a promise of value to be delivered. It articulates the specific benefits a customer can expect to receive from a company's products or services, and how those benefits differentiate the company from its competitors. A value proposition is not just a catchy slogan or a list of features; it is a strategic tool that connects a company's offerings to its customers' deepest needs and desires.

To be effective, a value proposition must possess several key elements. First and foremost, it must be clear and concise. A muddled or convoluted value proposition will fail to resonate with customers and will undermine the company's messaging efforts. Clarity is essential in communicating the core benefits and differentiators of a company's offerings.

Relevance is another critical component of a strong value proposition. It must speak directly to the needs, pain points, and aspirations of the target audience. A value proposition that fails to connect with customers on a meaningful level will struggle to gain traction in the market.

Differentiation is also vital. In today's crowded and noisy marketplace, a company's value proposition must set it apart from the competition. It should highlight the unique strengths and capabilities that enable the company to deliver superior value to its customers. Without a clear differentiator, a company risks being lost in the sea of sameness.

Finally, a value proposition must be credible. It should be grounded in reality and supported by evidence of the company's ability to deliver on its promises. Bold claims that lack substance will erode trust and undermine the effectiveness of the value proposition.

Some of the most successful companies in the world have built their success on the foundation of a compelling value proposition. Consider Apple's "Think Different" proposition, which encapsulated the company's commitment to innovation, creativity, and user-centric design. Or Walmart's "Save Money. Live Better." proposition, which speaks directly to the needs and aspirations of cost-conscious consumers. These value propositions are more than just slogans; they are strategic north stars that guide every aspect of the company's operations.

The benefits of a strong value proposition are manifold. First and foremost, it attracts and retains target customers. When a company's value proposition resonates with its audience, it creates a powerful bond of loyalty and advocacy. Customers who feel understood and well-served by a company are more likely to stick with it over time and recommend it to others.

A strong value proposition also differentiates a company from its competitors. In a world of endless choices, customers are drawn to companies that stand out from the crowd. A well-crafted value proposition can help a company carve out a distinct position in the market and build a competitive moat around its business.

Moreover, a value proposition provides a clear focus for the organization. It serves as a unifying force that aligns everyone around a common goal of delivering value to customers. This focus guides product development, ensuring that new offerings are designed to meet the needs and preferences of the target audience. It also informs marketing strategies, ensuring that messaging and campaigns are consistent and compelling.

So, how can a company go about crafting its own value proposition? The process begins with a deep understanding of the target customers. Who are they? What are their needs, desires, and pain points? What motivates and inspires them? Answering these questions requires a combination of market research, customer insights, and empathy.

Next, the company must identify its own unique strengths and differentiators. What capabilities, resources, or expertise set it apart from the competition? How can these strengths be leveraged to deliver superior value to customers? This introspection is critical in crafting a value proposition that is authentic and credible.

As the value proposition takes shape, it's important to ensure that it aligns with the company's overall vision and core values. A disconnect between the value proposition and the company's foundational principles will create confusion and undermine the effectiveness of both.

Articulating the value proposition in a clear, concise way is also crucial. This is where the art of messaging comes into play. The value proposition should be easy to understand, memorable, and emotionally resonant. It should also be flexible enough to be communicated across various touchpoints and channels, from the company website to sales conversations to advertising campaigns.

Once the value proposition is crafted, it must be tested and refined based on customer feedback. This iterative process helps ensure that the value proposition remains relevant and effective over time. It also allows the company to adapt to changing customer needs and market conditions.

Communicating and delivering the value proposition is just as important as crafting it. Consistency is key here. The value proposition should be woven into every aspect of the customer experience, from the first touchpoint to the post-purchase follow-up. All employees, from the front lines to the back office, should be equipped to communicate and deliver on the value proposition in their interactions with customers.

Marketing plays a critical role in communicating the value proposition to the broader market. Marketing messages and campaigns should be aligned with the value proposition, reinforcing its key themes and differentiators. Metrics should also be put in place to measure and monitor the effectiveness of the value proposition in driving customer acquisition, retention, and advocacy.

Of course, crafting and delivering a strong value proposition is not a one-and-done exercise. Customer needs and market trends are constantly evolving, and a company's value proposition must evolve with them. This requires a commitment to continuous innovation and improvement in products, services, and experiences.

At the same time, a company must be careful not to stray too far from its core value proposition. Consistency and credibility are key to building long-term trust and loyalty with customers. Balancing the need for adaptation with the need for consistency is an ongoing challenge that requires strategic discipline and customer-centric agility.

Of course, developing and executing a strong value proposition is not without its challenges. One common pitfall is crafting a value proposition that is too broad or generic, failing to differentiate the company from its competitors. Another is failing to align the value proposition with the actual customer experience, creating a gap between promise and reality.

Internal silos and resistance to change can also pose obstacles to a customer-centric value proposition. Breaking down these barriers requires strong leadership, cross-functional collaboration, and a shared commitment to putting the customer at the center of everything the company does.

Competitive pressures and market disruptions can also threaten a company's value proposition over time. Staying ahead of these challenges requires a combination of vigilance, agility, and a willingness to adapt and evolve while staying true to the company's core principles and differentiators.

In conclusion, crafting and delivering a compelling value proposition requires a deep understanding of customers, a clear sense of the company's unique strengths, and a commitment to consistency and continuous improvement. By aligning their value propositions with the principles of vision, core values, and customer centricity, companies can create a powerful, integrated strategy for delivering superior value to their customers.

Examples

Let's consider Warby Parker, the innovative eyewear company that has disrupted the traditional retail model. Founded in 2010, Warby Parker's value proposition is clear and compelling: "Designer eyewear at a revolutionary price." This simple statement encapsulates several key benefits that resonate deeply with the company's target audience of style-conscious, budget-minded consumers.

At the heart of Warby Parker's value proposition is a commitment to offering high-quality, stylish eyewear at a fraction of the price of traditional designer brands. By cutting out the middlemen and designing its frames in-house, Warby Parker is able to offer its customers a curated selection of fashionable glasses for just $95, including prescription lenses.

But Warby Parker's value proposition extends beyond just price. The company has also built a strong reputation for exceptional customer service, with a user-friendly website, free home try-on program, and no-questions-asked return policy. This customer-centric approach has earned Warby Parker a fiercely loyal following and a Net Promoter Score that rivals that of Apple.

Warby Parker's value proposition is also deeply aligned with its mission of doing good in the world. For every pair of glasses sold, the company donates a pair to someone in need through its Buy a Pair, Give a Pair program. This social impact component resonates with customers who are looking to make a positive difference with their purchases.

The results speak for themselves. In just over a decade, Warby Parker has grown from a scrappy startup to a beloved brand with over 100 retail locations and a valuation of over $3 billion. Its success is a testament to the power of a clear, compelling value proposition that aligns with customers' needs and values.

Another example of a company with a strong, successful value proposition is Slack, the team collaboration platform that has transformed the way work gets done. Slack's value proposition is summed up in its tagline: "Where work happens." This simple phrase speaks to the core benefit that Slack provides:

a centralized hub for communication, collaboration, and integration that boosts productivity and alignment.

For its target audience of fast-paced, tech-savvy teams, Slack's value proposition is a game-changer. By bringing together messaging, file sharing, and app integration in one user-friendly platform, Slack streamlines workflows and reduces the friction of context-switching. It's a far cry from the clunky, siloed communication tools of the past.

Slack's value proposition is also highly differentiated in a crowded market of collaboration tools. Its extensive app ecosystem, customizable integrations, and robust search capabilities set it apart from more basic messaging apps. And its playful, human brand voice resonates with users who are looking for a tool that feels more like a trusted teammate than a faceless software.

Like Warby Parker, Slack's value proposition is also aligned with a larger mission. The company's stated purpose is "to make people's working lives simpler, more pleasant, and more productive." This mission is reflected not just in the product itself, but in the company's culture of transparency, inclusivity, and customer-centricity.

The proof of Slack's value proposition is in its rapid adoption and growth. In just six years, Slack has grown to over 12 million daily active users and a valuation of over $20 billion. It has become the de facto communication tool for many of the world's most innovative and fast-moving companies.

These examples illustrate the power of a value proposition that is clear, relevant, differentiated, and aligned with a larger purpose. By deeply understanding their customers' needs and crafting a unique value offering that speaks directly to those needs, Warby Parker and Slack have built not just successful businesses, but beloved brands with fierce customer loyalty.

* * *

6

The Principle of Customer Segments

In business strategy, the Principle of Customer Segments stands as a critical pillar, guiding companies to understand and cater to the diverse needs of their target audiences. This principle emphasizes the importance of identifying, analyzing, and prioritizing different customer groups to develop tailored value propositions, products, services, and experiences that resonate with each segment. By embracing the Principle of Customer Segments, companies can unlock the key to building lasting customer relationships, driving growth, and securing a competitive edge in their markets.

At its core, the Principle of Customer Segments is rooted in the recognition that not all customers are the same. Every market consists of individuals and organizations with unique characteristics, needs, preferences, and behaviors. To succeed in today's complex and evolving business landscape, companies must move beyond a one-size-fits-all approach and instead adopt a customer-centric mindset that acknowledges and capitalizes on these differences.

The process of customer segmentation involves dividing the total market into smaller, more homogeneous groups based on shared attributes. These attributes can span a wide range of dimensions, including demographics (age, gender, income), psychographics (lifestyle, values, personality), behavior (purchase frequency, brand loyalty), and needs (functional, emotional, social). By analyzing these dimensions, companies can identify distinct segments that exhibit similar patterns and requirements, allowing for more targeted and effective business strategies.

Effective customer segmentation is an art and a science. It requires a deep understanding of the market, customers, and the company's own capabilities and objectives. To identify meaningful segments, companies must gather and analyze data from various sources, such as customer surveys, market research, sales records, and digital interactions. This data-driven approach enables companies to uncover insights into customer preferences, pain points, and decision-making processes, forming the foundation for segment definition.

Once segments are identified, companies must evaluate their attractiveness and viability. Not all segments are created equal, and some may offer greater potential for growth, profitability, and long-term value than others. To prioritize segments, companies should consider factors such as market size, growth rate, competition, and alignment with the company's strengths and strategic objectives. This strategic prioritization allows companies to focus their resources and efforts on the segments that are most likely to drive business success.

With priority segments identified, the next step is to develop tailored value propositions that align with the specific needs and preferences of each group. A value proposition is a clear, compelling statement of the unique benefits a company offers to its target customers. By crafting segment-specific value propositions, companies can communicate how their products, services, and experiences address the distinct requirements and aspirations of each customer group. This targeted approach resonates with customers, builds trust and loyalty, and sets the company apart from competitors who may offer more generic or undifferentiated offerings.

Customer segmentation also informs product development and innovation. By understanding the nuances of each segment, companies can design and deliver products and services that directly meet the needs and expectations of their target customers. This customer-centric approach to innovation ensures that the company's offerings remain relevant, valuable, and differentiated in the eyes of its chosen segments. Moreover, by involving customers in the innovation process through feedback, co-creation, and beta testing, companies can validate their assumptions, refine their offerings, and build anticipation and advocacy among their target audiences.

Marketing and communication strategies are another critical area where the Principle of Customer Segments comes into play. By tailoring marketing messages, channels, and tactics to the preferences and behaviors of each segment, companies can improve the effectiveness and efficiency of their outreach efforts. Segment-specific marketing allows companies to speak directly to the unique needs, aspirations, and challenges of each customer group, creating a sense of personalization and relevance that cuts through the noise of generic advertising. This targeted approach not only enhances customer engagement and conversion rates but also optimizes marketing spend by directing resources toward the channels and touchpoints that matter most to each segment.

Beyond external-facing strategies, the Principle of Customer Segments also has profound implications for organizational alignment and culture. By putting customer segments at the heart of the business, companies can foster a customer-centric mindset that permeates all levels and functions of the organization. This alignment ensures that every decision, from product development to customer service, is guided by a deep understanding of and commitment to the needs of each segment. A customer-centric culture also promotes cross-functional collaboration and breaks down silos, as teams work together to deliver seamless, tailored experiences that exceed customer expectations.

However, implementing the Principle of Customer Segments is not without its challenges. Segmentation requires significant investments in data collection, analysis, and interpretation. Companies must have the right tools, talent, and processes in place to turn raw data into actionable insights. Moreover, as customer needs and market conditions evolve, segments must be regularly reviewed and updated to ensure they remain relevant and effective. This ongoing refinement requires a commitment to continuous learning, experimentation, and adaptation.

Another challenge lies in balancing the benefits of segmentation with the costs and complexities of serving multiple customer groups. Companies must carefully evaluate the trade-offs between customization and scalability, ensuring that their segmentation strategies are both effective and sustainable in the long run. This may involve focusing on a select few high-priority segments, or finding ways to efficiently serve multiple segments through modular or configurable offerings.

Despite these challenges, the rewards of embracing the Principle of Customer Segments are substantial. By understanding and catering to the unique needs of different customer groups, companies can build deeper, more meaningful relationships that drive loyalty, advocacy, and long-term value. Segmentation also allows companies to identify and capitalize on new market opportunities, diversify their customer base, and mitigate the risks of overreliance on any single group.

Moreover, the insights gained through customer segmentation can inform and enhance other aspects of the business, such as pricing strategies, distribution channels, and partnerships. By aligning these elements with the needs and preferences of each segment, companies can create a holistic, customer-centric business model that delivers superior value and drives sustainable growth.

In conclusion, the Principle of Customer Segments is a powerful tool for building successful business strategies in today's complex and dynamic markets. By understanding and prioritizing the diverse needs of different customer groups, companies can develop tailored value propositions, products, services, and experiences that resonate with each segment. This customer-centric approach fosters loyalty, drives innovation, and sets the stage for long-term success.

Coca-Cola

Coca-Cola, the global beverage giant, has long been a master of customer segmentation. The company recognizes that its customers have diverse preferences, lifestyles, and needs, and it has developed a wide range of products and marketing strategies to cater to these different segments.

THE PRINCIPLE OF CUSTOMER SEGMENTS

One key segment for Coca-Cola is the health-conscious consumer. To appeal to this group, the company has developed a range of low-sugar and sugar-free options, such as Coca-Cola Zero and Diet Coke. These products are marketed with an emphasis on their taste and refreshment, while also highlighting their lower calorie content. Coca-Cola also targets this segment with its water and juice brands, such as Dasani and Minute Maid, positioning them as healthier alternatives to sugary drinks.

Another important segment for Coca-Cola is the youth market. To engage this segment, the company leverages music, sports, and social media partnerships to create experiences and content that resonate with younger consumers. For example, Coca-Cola has been a long-time sponsor of the Olympic Games, the FIFA World Cup, and various music festivals, using these platforms to connect with young people around shared passions and values. The company also develops youth-oriented marketing campaigns, such as the "Share a Coke" campaign, which featured popular names and phrases on Coca-Cola bottles to encourage personalization and sharing among friends.

Coca-Cola also recognizes the importance of cultural and geographic segmentation. The company tailors its products and marketing to the unique preferences and traditions of different countries and regions. For example, in China, Coca-Cola has developed localized flavors, such as Sprite Tea and Schweppes+ C Lemon, to cater to Chinese taste preferences. In Latin America, the company has a strong presence in the carbonated soft drink market, with a focus on larger, family-sized packaging to align with the region's cultural emphasis on shared meals and celebrations.

Coca-Cola's segmentation strategy also extends to occasion-based marketing. The company positions its products as the perfect accompaniment to various moments and experiences, from family dinners to sporting events to social gatherings. This occasion-based approach allows Coca-Cola to be a part of its customers' lives and memories, building an emotional connection that transcends the functional benefits of the product.

Apple

Apple, the iconic technology company, is another prime example of effective customer segmentation. Apple's products and marketing are carefully crafted to appeal to specific customer groups, each with their own needs, preferences, and aspirations.

One key segment for Apple is the creative professional. This includes designers, musicians, photographers, and filmmakers who rely on high-performance technology to bring their ideas to life. For this segment, Apple offers powerful, intuitive tools such as the MacBook Pro, iMac, and iPad Pro, along with specialized software like Final Cut Pro and Logic Pro. Apple's marketing to this segment emphasizes the performance, precision, and creativity that its products enable, positioning them as essential tools for professional-grade work.

Another important segment for Apple is the affluent, tech-savvy consumer. This group values style, status, and innovation, and is willing to pay a premium for cutting-edge features and design. Apple caters to this segment with its flagship iPhone and Apple Watch lines, which combine advanced technology with luxury materials and craftsmanship. Apple's marketing to this segment emphasizes the prestige and exclusivity of its products, with sleek, aspirational imagery and messaging that highlights the latest features and capabilities.

Apple also targets the education market, recognizing the importance of introducing its products and ecosystem to students and educators. The company offers discounted pricing and specialized software packages for schools and universities, promoting the use of iPads and Macs as powerful learning tools. By engaging students early on, Apple aims to build long-term loyalty and advocacy, as these customers carry their preferences and habits into their personal and professional lives.

In recent years, Apple has also focused on the health and wellness segment. With the launch of the Apple Watch and the expansion of its Health app, Apple has positioned itself as a partner in its customers' wellness journeys. The company's marketing to this segment emphasizes the health tracking, fitness coaching, and mindfulness features of its products, aligning with the growing consumer interest in self-care and preventive health.

Across all its segments, Apple maintains a consistent brand identity and value proposition centered on innovation, design, and user experience. The company's sleek, minimalist aesthetics and intuitive interfaces appeal to customers who value simplicity and ease of use, while its ecosystem of integrated hardware, software, and services creates a seamless, immersive experience that keeps customers engaged and loyal.

Apple's segmentation strategy has been a key driver of its success, allowing the company to create products and experiences that deeply resonate with its target customers. By understanding and catering to the unique needs and aspirations of each segment, Apple has built a passionate, dedicated customer base that extends far beyond the functional benefits of its products. This emotional connection, combined with Apple's relentless focus on innovation and design, has made it one of the most valuable and influential brands in the world.

* * *

7

The Principle of Focus

In the fast-paced, ever-changing world of business, it's easy to get caught up in the pursuit of growth and opportunity at all costs. Companies are constantly tempted to expand into new markets, launch new products, and chase after every shiny object that catches their eye. But in the midst of all this chaos and complexity, there is a simple and powerful principle that separates truly great companies from the rest: the Principle of Focus.

At its core, the Principle of Focus is about clarity and discipline. It's about having a deep understanding of who you are as a company, what you stand for, and what you're uniquely positioned to do better than anyone else. It's about making tough choices and trade-offs, saying no to some opportunities so that you can say a resounding yes to others. And it's about aligning every aspect of your organization – your people, your processes, your resources – around a clear and compelling strategic vision.

The Principle of Focus starts with a simple but profound question: What is your company's core focus? What is the one thing that you do better than anyone else, that delivers the most value to your customers, and that drives your competitive advantage? This core focus should be rooted in your company's unique strengths, capabilities, and assets. It should be something that you're deeply passionate about and that aligns with your values and purpose as an organization.

Once you've identified your core focus, the next step is to ruthlessly prioritize it above all else. This means making hard choices about what you will and won't do as a company. It means being willing to say no to opportunities that don't fit with your strategic focus, even if they seem attractive or lucrative in the short term. It means investing disproportionately in the areas that are most critical to your success, even if it means under-investing in others.

One company that embodies the Principle of Focus is Apple. From its earliest days, Apple has been laser-focused on creating beautifully designed, easy-to-use products that delight customers and transform industries. This focus has guided every aspect of Apple's strategy and decision-making over the years, from its product development to its marketing to its retail experiences.

Apple's focus has meant making some tough trade-offs along the way. The company has been famously selective about the products it chooses to develop, often saying no to seemingly promising opportunities in order to maintain its strategic clarity. It has also been willing to cannibalize its own products when necessary, launching new innovations that make its older offerings obsolete. These trade-offs have not always been easy, but they have been essential to Apple's long-term success.

Another company that demonstrates the power of focus is Southwest Airlines. Since its founding in 1971, Southwest has had a singular focus on being the low-cost leader in the airline industry. This focus has guided every aspect of Southwest's business model, from its point-to-point route structure to its no-frills service to its standardized fleet of Boeing 737 aircraft.

Southwest's focus on low costs has allowed it to consistently offer lower fares than its competitors, attracting a loyal customer base and driving profitable growth even in tough economic times. It has also given Southwest a clear identity and brand promise that sets it apart in a crowded and commoditized industry. By staying true to its core focus, Southwest has become one of the most successful and admired companies in the world.

The Principle of Focus is not just about strategy; it's also about execution. Once you've defined your core focus, you need to align every aspect of your organization around delivering on that focus with excellence. This means building a culture and team that is passionate about your core focus and that has the skills and capabilities to execute it flawlessly. It means designing processes and systems that are optimized for your core focus, and that eliminate any unnecessary complexity or distraction. And it means allocating your resources – your time, your money, your people – in a way that supports and amplifies your core focus.

One of the biggest challenges in maintaining focus is the constant temptation to chase after shiny objects and new opportunities. In today's fast-moving business environment, it's easy to get seduced by the latest trend or the hottest new market. But the most successful companies are the ones that have the discipline to stay true to their core focus, even in the face of temptation.

This doesn't mean that companies should never evolve or adapt to changing circumstances. In fact, the ability to pivot and respond to new challenges and opportunities is essential to long-term success. But the key is to make sure that any changes or additions to your strategy are aligned with and supportive of your core focus. If a new opportunity doesn't fit with your core focus, or if it would require you to dilute or compromise that focus, then it's probably not the right opportunity for you.

Another key aspect of the Principle of Focus is communication. It's not enough to simply have a clear and compelling focus; you also need to communicate that focus clearly and consistently to all of your stakeholders. This includes your employees, who need to understand how their work contributes to the company's core focus and strategy. It includes your customers, who need to know what sets your company apart and why they should choose you over the competition. And it includes your investors, who need to understand your strategic direction and how it will create long-term value.

Effective communication of your core focus requires a strong and consistent brand identity. Your brand should be a clear and compelling expression of your core focus, conveying the unique value that you offer to your customers and the world. It should be reflected in everything from your visual identity to your messaging to your customer experiences. And it should be reinforced through every touchpoint and interaction that your stakeholders have with your company.

Ultimately, the Principle of Focus is about creating a virtuous cycle of clarity, alignment, and excellence. When you have a clear and compelling core focus, it allows you to make better strategic choices and trade-offs. This in turn allows you to align your organization more effectively around your strategy, creating a culture of focus and discipline. And when your entire organization is aligned and focused on delivering your core value proposition with excellence, it creates a powerful competitive advantage that is difficult for others to replicate.

Of course, maintaining focus is not always easy. It requires constant vigilance and discipline, and a willingness to make tough choices and trade-offs. It also requires a deep understanding of your customers, your market, and your own capabilities, as well as a willingness to adapt and evolve as circumstances change.

But for those companies that are able to master the Principle of Focus, the rewards are immense. They are able to create a powerful and enduring brand identity, build deep and loyal customer relationships, and deliver superior financial performance over the long term. They are able to attract and retain the best talent, foster a culture of innovation and excellence, and make a positive impact on the world around them.

Focus vs Vision and Value Proposition

Vision is the overarching, long-term aspiration and purpose of the company. It's the guiding star that sets the direction and inspires the organization towards a desired future state.

Value Proposition, on the other hand, is the unique set of benefits and experiences that a company offers to its customers. It's the reason why customers should choose your products or services over those of your competitors.

Focus, in contrast, is about the strategic choices and trade-offs a company makes to align its resources and activities around delivering on its Value

Proposition and achieving its Vision. It's about saying no to certain opportunities or activities in order to excel at the things that are most critical to success.

In simpler terms:

- Vision is the destination
- Value Proposition is the vehicle
- Focus is the route you choose to get there

A clear Vision and compelling Value Proposition are essential foundations, but without Focus, a company risks getting lost along the way, chasing too many distractions or spreading itself too thin.

Ultimately, all three concepts work together in harmony. The Vision guides the Value Proposition, the Value Proposition defines the Focus, and the Focus enables the realization of the Vision. By understanding and aligning these key elements, companies can create a powerful and cohesive strategy for long-term success.

Amazon

One company that has masterfully embodied the Principle of Focus throughout its history is Amazon. From its humble beginnings as an online bookseller to its current position as one of the world's most valuable and influential companies, Amazon has maintained a laser-like focus on a few key strategic priorities that have guided its growth and evolution over the years.

Amazon's core focus can be summed up in its mission statement: "To be Earth's most customer-centric company, where customers can find and discover anything they might want to buy online, and endeavors to offer its customers the lowest possible prices." This statement reflects Amazon's relentless focus on two key pillars: customer experience and operational efficiency.

In terms of customer experience, Amazon has always been obsessed with understanding and serving the needs of its customers better than anyone else. This focus has guided every aspect of Amazon's business, from its product selection to its website design to its delivery and customer service. Amazon has consistently invested in new technologies and capabilities that enhance the customer experience, such as personalized recommendations, one-click ordering, and Prime shipping. It has also been willing to experiment with new business models and offerings, such as Amazon Web Services and Amazon Prime Video, that extend its value proposition and deepen its customer relationships.

At the same time, Amazon has been equally focused on driving operational efficiency and cost leadership. This focus has allowed Amazon to offer lower prices and faster delivery than its competitors, creating a powerful competitive advantage. Amazon has invested heavily in its logistics and fulfillment capabilities, building a vast network of warehouses and delivery vehicles that allow it to get products to customers quickly and cheaply. It has also leveraged technology and data analytics to optimize every aspect of its operations, from inventory management to product placement to pricing.

One of the keys to Amazon's success has been its willingness to make bold bets and investments in service of its core focus. For example, when Amazon launched Amazon Prime in 2005, many observers were skeptical that customers would pay an annual fee for free shipping. But Amazon believed that Prime would enhance the customer experience and drive long-term loyalty, and it invested heavily in the program despite short-term financial losses. Today, Prime has over 150 million members worldwide and is one of Amazon's most powerful competitive advantages.

Another example of Amazon's focus in action is its approach to product development. Rather than trying to be all things to all people, Amazon has been selective about the product categories it enters and the offerings it develops. It has focused on areas where it can leverage its core strengths in customer experience and operational efficiency, such as e-books, cloud computing, and voice assistants. And it has been willing to discontinue or de-emphasize products that don't fit with its strategic priorities, such as its Fire Phone smartphone.

Perhaps most importantly, Amazon's focus has been deeply ingrained in its culture and leadership. From CEO Jeff Bezos on down, Amazon's leaders have consistently emphasized the importance of customer obsession, long-term thinking, and operational excellence. They have made tough choices and trade-offs in service of these priorities, even when it meant sacrificing short-term profits or facing criticism from investors. And they have communicated these priorities clearly and consistently to all of Amazon's stakeholders, from its employees to its customers to its shareholders.

In the end, by identifying and relentlessly pursuing a clear and compelling strategic focus, Amazon has been able to create immense value for its customers, its employees, and its shareholders. It has built one of the world's most valuable and admired brands, and it has transformed entire industries and economies in the process.

* * *

8

The Principle of Differentiation

In the fiercely competitive landscape of modern business, standing out from the crowd is no longer a luxury – it's a necessity. With countless companies vying for the attention and loyalty of customers, the ability to differentiate oneself has become a fundamental prerequisite for success. This is where the Principle of Differentiation comes into play.

At its core, differentiation is about creating a unique and compelling identity for your company, one that sets you apart from your rivals and resonates deeply with your target customers. It's about carving out a distinct position in the market and offering something of value that others cannot easily replicate.

While the concept of differentiation is closely related to the ideas of Focus and Value Proposition, which we've explored in earlier chapters, it goes beyond simply choosing a target customer or articulating a set of benefits. Differentiation is about the holistic way in which a company presents itself to the world – the sum total of its products, services, experiences, and brand identity that make it truly one-of-a-kind.

So why is differentiation so critical to business success? In a word, it's about competitive advantage. When a company is able to establish a clear and compelling point of difference in the market, it gives customers a reason to choose them over others. It allows the company to escape the trap of commoditization, where products and services become interchangeable and pricing becomes the primary basis for competition.

Differentiation also enables companies to build deeper, more loyal relationships with customers. When customers perceive a company as uniquely suited to their needs and preferences, they are more likely to stick with that company over time, even in the face of competing offers. This loyalty translates into higher customer lifetime value, more stable revenue streams, and a more resilient business overall.

Moreover, differentiation can help companies command a price premium for their offerings. When customers perceive a company's products or services as distinctly better or more valuable than the alternatives, they are often willing to pay more for them. This allows the company to boost margins, reinvest in innovation and growth, and create a virtuous cycle of value creation.

Crafting Your Differentiation Strategy

The first step in crafting a differentiation strategy is to develop a deep understanding of your target customers. What are their needs, preferences, and pain points? What motivates and inspires them? What do they value most in the products and services they buy? By gaining insight into the hearts and minds of your customers, you can begin to identify opportunities to serve them in unique and compelling ways.

Next, it's important to assess your company's own unique strengths and capabilities. What do you do particularly well? What assets, resources, or competencies set you apart from your competitors? These could include things like proprietary technology, deep industry expertise, exceptional customer service, or a powerful brand identity. By leveraging your distinctive strengths, you can create a differentiation strategy that is authentic, sustainable, and difficult for others to imitate.

Once you've identified your target customers and your unique strengths, the next step is to craft a clear and compelling Value Proposition that brings them together. This involves articulating the specific benefits and experiences that you offer to customers, and how they are uniquely tailored to their needs and preferences. Your Value Proposition should be concise, memorable, and emotionally resonant – a simple yet powerful statement of the value you deliver and the difference you make in customers' lives.

Importantly, your Value Proposition must also be supported by a coherent and integrated set of strategic choices across your entire business. This means aligning your product and service offerings, your pricing and distribution strategies, your marketing and branding efforts, and your organizational capabilities and culture around delivering on your differentiated promise. Every touchpoint and interaction that customers have with your company should reinforce and amplify your unique identity and value.

Differentiation in Action

To bring the Principle of Differentiation to life, let's consider a few real-world examples of companies that have successfully carved out distinct positions in their markets.

One classic example is Apple. From its early days, Apple has differentiated itself through its focus on design, usability, and customer experience. Its products are known for their sleek and intuitive interfaces, their seamless integration with other Apple devices and services, and their premium brand identity. By consistently delivering on this differentiated promise, Apple has cultivated a fiercely loyal customer base and a highly profitable business model.

Another example is Southwest Airlines. In an industry notorious for commoditization and price competition, Southwest has differentiated itself through its unique business model and customer experience. With its point-to-point route network, its single-class cabins, and its fun and friendly service, Southwest has created a distinct identity as the low-cost, no-frills carrier that puts customers first. This differentiation has allowed Southwest to build a strong and profitable business in the face of intense competition.

A third example is Patagonia, the outdoor clothing and gear company. Patagonia has differentiated itself through its commitment to environmental and social responsibility, as well as its high-quality, durable products. By aligning its entire business around its core values of sustainability, transparency, and activism, Patagonia has built a powerful brand identity that resonates deeply with its target customers. This differentiation has allowed Patagonia to command premium prices, foster intense customer loyalty, and make a positive impact on the world.

Overcoming the Challenges of Differentiation

Differentiation is not without its challenges. In today's fast-moving and hyper-competitive business environment, it can be difficult to establish and maintain a truly unique position in the market. Competitors are constantly looking for ways to imitate or outflank successful differentiators, and customer needs and preferences are always evolving.

To overcome these challenges, companies must be relentless in their pursuit of continuous improvement and innovation. They must constantly seek out new ways to enhance their unique value proposition, whether through product development, service enhancements, or brand building. They must also stay close to their customers, continuously gathering feedback and insights to stay attuned to their changing needs and expectations.

Another key challenge of differentiation is the need for consistency and alignment across the organization. It's not enough to simply articulate a differentiated Value Proposition – every aspect of the business must be geared towards delivering on that promise. This requires strong leadership, clear communication, and a culture of customer centricity and innovation.

Lululemon

Founded in 1998 in Vancouver, Canada, Lululemon has grown to become a global brand with a passionate and loyal following. Key to Lululemon's success has been its ability to differentiate itself in the highly competitive sportswear market.

Lululemon's core differentiation lies in its focus on creating high-quality, performance-driven products that inspire people to live healthy and active lives. Unlike many of its competitors, who focus primarily on sports and athletics, Lululemon has positioned itself as a lifestyle brand that embodies the values of mindfulness, wellness, and personal growth.

One of the key ways Lululemon differentiates itself is through its innovative product design. The company uses proprietary fabrics and technologies, such as its signature Luon fabric, to create products that are both functional and comfortable. Lululemon's products are designed with the needs of yoga practitioners and athletes in mind, featuring details like flat seams, moisture-wicking properties, and four-way stretch. This attention to detail and performance has helped Lululemon establish a reputation for quality and innovation in the market.

Another key aspect of Lululemon's differentiation strategy is its focus on community and customer experience. The company is known for its in-store yoga classes, running clubs, and other events that bring customers together and foster a sense of belonging. Lululemon's store associates, known as "educators," are trained to provide personalized service and expertise to help customers find the right products for their needs. This emphasis on community and customer experience has helped Lululemon build a fiercely loyal customer base that sees the brand as more than just a place to buy clothes.

Lululemon has also differentiated itself through its commitment to sustainability and social responsibility. The company uses sustainable materials in many of its products, such as recycled polyester and responsibly-sourced wool, and has set ambitious targets for reducing its environmental footprint. Lululemon also partners with organizations that support yoga, mindfulness, and personal development, aligning its brand with positive social impact.

Importantly, Lululemon's differentiation strategy is deeply integrated across its entire business model. From product design and merchandising to store operations and community engagement, every aspect of the company is geared towards delivering on its unique value proposition. This alignment has allowed Lululemon to create a powerful and cohesive brand identity that resonates deeply with its target customers.

The results of Lululemon's differentiation strategy have been impressive. The company has achieved consistent growth and profitability, even in the face of intense competition from larger sportswear brands. Lululemon's loyal customers are willing to pay premium prices for its products, giving the company a strong and defensible market position. And the brand's reputation for quality, innovation, and social impact has helped it expand into new product categories and geographic markets.

***

9

The Principle of Core Competencies

In the world of business strategy, the principle of core competencies emerges as one of the fundamental concepts that can significantly impact an organization's success. This principle focuses on identifying, nurturing, and exploiting the unique blend of skills, knowledge, and resources that differentiate a company from its rivals.

Core competencies go beyond mere strengths; they are the deeply embedded capabilities that shape a company's identity, guide its operations, and provide a foundation for sustainable competitive advantage. These competencies arise from the collective learning, knowledge sharing, and the seamless integration of various technologies and production skills within the organization.

A prime example of core competencies in action is Toyota's renowned Toyota Production System (TPS). This lean manufacturing system, developed through years of continuous improvement and refinement, embodies Toyota's core competencies in quality management, process optimization, and employee engagement. TPS is not merely a collection of tools and techniques, but a philosophy that permeates every aspect of the organization.

Central to TPS is the concept of "Kaizen," or continuous improvement. This core competency is deeply rooted in Toyota's culture, empowering every employee to identify and eliminate waste, streamline processes, and enhance quality. By fostering a culture of continuous improvement and employee ownership, Toyota has developed a resilient and adaptable organization that consistently outperforms its competitors in terms of efficiency, reliability, and customer satisfaction.

Another company that has successfully harnessed its core competencies is Apple. While Apple is renowned for its innovative products, its true core competencies lie in design thinking, user experience, and ecosystem management. Apple's products are not only visually appealing but also intuitive and seamlessly integrated, supported by a robust ecosystem of software, services, and third-party applications.

Apple's core competency in design thinking is evident in its product development process. The company begins by deeply understanding user needs and desires, then works backwards to create products that address those needs in a way that is both functional and emotionally engaging. This user-centric approach has enabled Apple to develop products that not only solve problems but also elicit joy and loyalty among customers.

Similarly, Apple's core competency in ecosystem management has been a significant driver of its success. By meticulously curating and controlling every aspect of the user experience – from hardware to software to content – Apple has created a "walled garden" that keeps users engaged and invested in its products and services. This ecosystem lock-in creates a high barrier to entry for competitors, providing Apple with a sustainable competitive advantage.

Developing and nurturing core competencies requires ongoing investment, experimentation, and learning. Companies must be willing to allocate resources – both financial and human – to areas that may not yield immediate results but have the potential to create long-term value. This long-term perspective is exemplified by Amazon's relentless focus on innovation and customer-centricity. Amazon's core competencies in logistics, data analytics, and platform management have been developed through years of experimentation and iteration.

However, identifying and developing core competencies is not without its challenges. In a rapidly evolving business landscape, what constitutes a core competency today may become irrelevant or obsolete tomorrow. Companies must, therefore, remain vigilant in monitoring market trends, customer preferences, and technological advancements, and be willing to adapt their core competencies accordingly.

To avoid the trap of spreading resources too thin and trying to be good at everything, organizations must be disciplined in identifying their core competencies and allocating resources accordingly. This means making tough decisions to say no to opportunities that do not align with the company's core strengths, even if they seem profitable in the short term. It also involves continuously reassessing and refining the company's core competencies, discarding those that no longer create value, and investing in those with the greatest potential for future growth.

Furthermore, successful companies recognize that core competencies must create value for customers. A core competency that does not translate into a meaningful benefit for the end-user is ultimately a wasted effort. Companies must ensure that their core competencies align with customer needs and preferences and that they are effectively communicated through marketing and branding efforts.

In conclusion, by identifying, developing, and leveraging the unique capabilities that set them apart from competitors, companies can create sustainable competitive advantages and drive long-term success.

***

10

The Principle of Strategic Activities

In business strategy, the principle of strategic activities holds a pivotal position. This concept emphasizes the importance of carefully selecting and executing a set of interconnected actions that enable a company to achieve its strategic objectives and create a sustainable competitive advantage.

At its core, the principle of strategic activities is about making deliberate choices. It involves identifying the key activities that are most critical to a company's success and focusing resources on executing those activities exceptionally well. By doing so, companies can differentiate themselves from competitors, deliver superior value to customers, and capture a larger share of the market.

One of the most powerful examples of strategic activities in action is Southwest Airlines. From its inception, Southwest chose to focus on a specific set of activities that set it apart from other airlines. These activities included:

1. **Point-to-point route structure:** Southwest flies directly between smaller cities, avoiding the hub-and-spoke model used by most major airlines. This allows for faster turnaround times and more efficient operations.
2. **No frills service:** Southwest forgoes traditional airline amenities like first-class seating, in-flight meals, and assigned seating. This simplicity reduces costs and allows the airline to offer lower fares.

3. **Single aircraft type:** Southwest operates an all-Boeing 737 fleet, which simplifies maintenance, training, and operations. This standardization leads to greater efficiency and cost savings.
4. **Quick turnaround times:** Southwest has honed its ground operations to minimize the time planes spend at the gate. Faster turnarounds mean more flights per day and better asset utilization.

By focusing on this specific set of activities, Southwest has been able to consistently offer low fares, maintain high levels of customer satisfaction, and achieve profitability in an industry known for its thin margins and intense competition.

Choosing the right strategic activities is not a one-time exercise; it requires ongoing assessment and adaptation. As market conditions change and new opportunities emerge, companies must be willing to recalibrate their activities to stay ahead of the curve.

Consider the example of Netflix. When Netflix first launched, its primary strategic activity was DVD rental by mail and the supported logistics system. However, as streaming technology advanced and consumer preferences shifted, Netflix made a bold decision to pivot towards online streaming. This shift required substantial investments in technology, content licensing, and original programming. By embracing this new set of strategic activities, Netflix was able to disrupt the entertainment industry and become a global leader in video streaming.

The principle of strategic activities is closely linked to the concept of trade-offs, which is explored in the next chapter. In order to excel at a specific set of activities, companies often have to make difficult choices about what not to do. This means foregoing certain opportunities or markets in order to focus resources on the activities that matter most.

For example, when Apple decided to enter the smartphone market with the iPhone, it made a strategic trade-off to focus on the high-end, premium segment. This meant foregoing the low-cost, mass-market approach that some competitors were pursuing. By making this trade-off and focusing its activities on delivering a superior user experience, Apple was able to capture a significant share of the high-end smartphone market and generate industry-leading profit margins.

Making trade-offs and focusing on strategic activities also requires a deep understanding of a company's unique strengths and capabilities. It involves playing to one's strengths and not trying to be all things to all people.

This is exemplified by the luxury fashion brand Hermès. Hermès is known for its exquisite craftsmanship, timeless designs, and uncompromising quality. The company's strategic activities are centered around preserving traditional artisanal skills, sourcing the finest materials, and maintaining a highly exclusive distribution network. By focusing on these activities and not diluting its brand with mass-market offerings, Hermès has been able to command premium prices and maintain a loyal customer base for generations.

However, executing strategic activities is not just about operational excellence; it's also about creating a unique and compelling value proposition for customers. A company's activities must work together to deliver something that customers truly value and are willing to pay for.

This is where the concept of strategic fit comes into play, which will be explored in more detail in the next chapter. In essence, strategic fit refers to the alignment and coherence between a company's various activities. When activities are well-aligned and mutually reinforcing, they create a whole that is greater than the sum of its parts.

Ultimately, the companies that master the principle of strategic activities are those that are able to create a virtuous cycle of value creation and capture. By consistently executing a well-aligned set of activities, they are able to deliver something truly unique and valuable to customers. This, in turn, leads to greater customer loyalty, higher profit margins, and a more defensible competitive position over time.

Examples

Zara

Zara, founded in 1975, has grown to become one of the world's largest fashion retailers, with over 2,200 stores in 96 countries. The company's success can be attributed to its unique business model, which is built on a foundation of core competencies, followed by strategic activities that enable it to respond quickly to changing fashion trends and customer preferences.

Core Competencies:

1. **Agile supply chain management:** Zara's most significant core competency is its highly responsive and vertically integrated supply chain. The company has developed a sophisticated system that allows it to design, produce, and distribute new clothing styles in a matter of weeks, rather than the months it takes traditional retailers. This agility enables Zara to quickly adapt to changing fashion trends and customer demands, minimizing the risk of unsold inventory.
2. **In-house design and production:** Another core competency that sets Zara apart is its in-house design and production capabilities. The company employs a team of over 700 designers who create new styles based on real-time feedback from store managers and customers. Zara also owns and operates its own production facilities, which allows it to maintain strict quality control and quickly produce small batches of new designs.
3. **Customer-centric retail experience:** Zara has developed a core competency in creating a unique and engaging retail experience for its customers. The company invests heavily in prime store locations, attractive visual merchandising, and attentive customer service. Zara's stores are designed to encourage customers to visit frequently, as new styles are introduced twice a week, creating a sense of scarcity and urgency.

By leveraging these core competencies, Zara has been able to execute a highly effective business strategy that has disrupted the traditional fashion retail model.

Strategic Activities:

1. **Rapid product development and introduction:** Zara's agile supply chain and in-house design capabilities enable the company to introduce new styles rapidly. The company can take a new design from concept to store shelves in as little as two weeks, allowing it to capitalize on the latest fashion trends and customer preferences.
2. **Limited production runs and frequent inventory turnover:** Zara produces smaller batches of each design, which creates a sense of exclusivity and scarcity. This approach encourages customers to make purchases quickly, as they know that popular styles may sell out fast. The company also introduces new styles frequently, which drives repeat visits and keeps the brand top-of-mind for fashion-conscious consumers.
3. **Real-time data collection and analysis:** Zara collects real-time data from its stores, including sales figures, customer feedback, and observations from store managers. This information is quickly fed back to the design and production teams, allowing them to adjust their plans and respond to changing market conditions. By continuously monitoring and adapting to customer preferences, Zara can minimize the risk of unsold inventory and maintain its reputation for being on-trend.
4. **Strategic store locations and layouts:** Zara carefully selects prime store locations in high-traffic areas and designs its stores to maximize visual appeal and customer engagement. The company frequently updates its store layouts and visual merchandising to showcase new styles and create an immersive shopping experience.

Zara's ability to consistently execute these strategic activities is rooted in its strong core competencies, which have been developed and refined over many years.

As Zara continues to expand globally, it will need to adapt its core competencies and strategic activities to new markets and changing customer preferences. However, by staying true to its fundamental strengths and maintaining its focus on agility and customer-centricity, Zara is well-positioned to remain a leader in the fast-fashion industry for years to come.

Starbucks

Founded in 1971 in Seattle, Washington, Starbucks has grown to become the world's largest coffeehouse chain, with more than 30,000 stores in 80 countries. The company's success can be attributed to its strong core competencies and set of strategic activities, which have enabled it to create a unique coffee culture and build a loyal customer base.

Core Competencies:

- **Coffee expertise, quality, and roasting:** Starbucks has a deep knowledge of coffee sourcing, roasting, and brewing, which allows it to consistently deliver high-quality coffee to its customers. The company's founders and employees are well-versed in the art of coffee roasting, which is a critical capability that sets Starbucks apart from its competitors.
- **Brand and customer experience:** Starbucks has built a strong brand identity that is associated with quality, convenience, and a welcoming atmosphere. The company's stores are designed to provide a comfortable and inviting "third place" between home and work, where customers can relax, socialize, or work.
- **Barista training and customer education:** Starbucks invests heavily in barista training to ensure that its employees have the skills and knowledge to create the perfect cup of coffee and provide excellent customer service. The company also focuses on educating customers about coffee, helping them appreciate and enjoy the beverage, which has contributed to its business growth.
- **Supply chain management:** Starbucks has a robust supply chain system

that follows a hub-and-spoke model. The company owns and operates its own roasting facilities, ensuring complete control over the quality of its coffee beans. Starbucks has long-term, fixed-price contracts with high-quality coffee growers from prominent locations, giving it a first-mover advantage and a reliable supply of premium coffee.

- **Technological innovation:** Starbucks has embraced digital technology to enhance the customer experience and streamline its operations. The company's mobile app and loyalty program allow customers to easily order, pay, and earn rewards, while also providing valuable data on customer preferences and behavior.
- **Culture and employee development:** Starbucks has a strong organizational culture that emphasizes diversity, inclusion, and personal growth. The company invests heavily in employee training and development, offering comprehensive benefits and opportunities for career advancement.

Strategic Activities:

- **Product innovation and customization:** Starbucks continuously innovates its product offerings to meet changing customer tastes and preferences. The company introduces new coffee blends, seasonal beverages, and food items, while also allowing customers to customize their orders.
- **Store expansion and global presence:** Starbucks has pursued an aggressive store expansion strategy, opening new locations in key markets around the world. The company adapts its store designs and menu offerings to local cultures and preferences, while maintaining a consistent brand identity.
- **Channel diversification:** In addition to its retail stores, Starbucks has expanded into other channels, such as grocery stores, airports, and universities. The company also offers a range of products, including packaged coffee, tea, and ready-to-drink beverages, which are sold through various distribution channels.
- **Real Estate Strategy:** Starbucks' real estate strategy is a strategic activity

that involves clustering stores in important locations to increase brand awareness, capture market share, and ultimately saturate the market. This approach allows Starbucks to maximize brand visibility, manage store traffic effectively, and maintain speedy service by distributing customer traffic across multiple nearby locations. By carefully selecting store locations based on demographic, economic, and cultural factors, Starbucks can adapt its offerings and store designs to meet the specific needs and preferences of each market. This strategic activity enables Starbucks to leverage its core competencies, such as brand strength and customer experience, to achieve its business objectives of growth, market dominance, and customer satisfaction, while making its stores more accessible and convenient for customers in key markets.

- **Procurement process:** Starbucks never outsources its procurement process, allowing it to maintain strict control over the quality of its coffee beans. The company has direct interactions with growers and adheres to stringent sourcing and social responsibility standards, making suppliers feel like an integral part of the Starbucks corporation.
- **Distribution center management:** Starbucks owns and controls some of its distribution centers, while others are operated by carefully vetted private partners. The company closely monitors the productivity and contract rates of its distribution centers using a 'scorecard' system, which provides outputs in terms of service metrics, cost metrics, and productivity metrics.
- **Social responsibility and sustainability:** Starbucks has made social responsibility and sustainability a key part of its business strategy. The company invests in ethical sourcing practices, environmental conservation, and community development programs. This includes long-term contracts with farming communities, providing them with stability and support.

By focusing on coffee quality, technological innovation, and employee development, Starbucks has been able to create a unique brand identity and maintain a competitive advantage in the global coffee industry.

STRATEGY IKIGAI

* * *

11

The Principle of Tradeoffs

In business strategy, the principle of tradeoffs is a critical concept that every successful organization must embrace. At its core, this principle acknowledges that no company can be everything to everyone. To achieve sustainable success, businesses must make deliberate choices about what they will and will not do, accepting that these decisions come with both benefits and costs.

The notion of tradeoffs is closely tied to the principle of focus, as discussed in one of the previous chapters. When a company decides to focus on a specific target market, value proposition, or set of core competencies, it inevitably forgoes other opportunities. This is the essence of strategic tradeoffs: consciously choosing to excel in certain areas while accepting limitations in others.

One of the most famous examples of strategic tradeoffs is the case of Southwest Airlines. From its inception, Southwest chose to prioritize low costs, high efficiency, and excellent customer service within the specific context of short-haul, point-to-point flights. To achieve these goals, the company made several key tradeoffs:

1. Southwest opted for a single aircraft type (Boeing 737) to minimize maintenance and training costs, even though this meant sacrificing the flexibility to serve certain routes or airports.

2. The airline chose not to offer assigned seating, in-flight meals, or interline baggage transfers, allowing for faster turnarounds and lower overhead costs.
3. Southwest focused on secondary airports and avoided major hubs, trading off some potential customers for lower operating costs and less congestion.

These tradeoffs allowed Southwest to develop a highly efficient, low-cost business model that has been consistently profitable for decades, despite the turbulence in the airline industry.

Another instructive example comes from the retail sector. Discount stores like Aldi and Lidl have made strategic tradeoffs that set them apart from traditional supermarkets. They offer a limited assortment of primarily private-label products, displayed in a no-frills environment with minimal staffing. By sacrificing variety and amenities, these retailers can offer significantly lower prices, appealing to a specific customer segment that prioritizes cost savings over choice and convenience.

In the technology industry, Apple is known for its focus on design, user experience, and ecosystem integration. To maintain this focus, Apple has made tradeoffs such as limiting customization options, maintaining a closed software ecosystem, and pricing its products at a premium. While these choices may deter some potential customers, they have allowed Apple to cultivate a loyal user base and maintain industry-leading profit margins.

However, making strategic tradeoffs is not without its challenges. It requires a deep understanding of the market, the competition, and the company's own capabilities. Tradeoffs must be based on sound data and analysis rather than intuition or guesswork. Organizations must also be prepared to communicate their tradeoffs clearly and consistently to both internal and external stakeholders, ensuring that everyone understands the reasoning behind these choices.

Another challenge is the temptation to compromise or hedge bets, trying to appeal to multiple customer segments or offer a wide range of products and services. This approach can be seductive, as it seems to minimize risk and maximize potential revenue. However, it often leads to a lack of differentiation, higher costs, and ultimately, subpar performance. As the saying goes, "If you try to be everything to everyone, you'll end up being nothing to no one."

To avoid this pitfall, companies must have the discipline to say "no" to opportunities that do not align with their strategic tradeoffs. This can be difficult, especially when faced with pressure from stakeholders or the allure of short-term gains. However, consistently adhering to a well-defined set of tradeoffs is essential for maintaining focus and building a sustainable competitive advantage.

In conclusion, the principle of tradeoffs requires companies to make deliberate choices about what they will and will not do, accepting the inherent limitations and costs of these decisions. By embracing tradeoffs, organizations can develop a clear focus, differentiate themselves from competitors, and allocate their resources more effectively. While making tradeoffs can be challenging, the rewards – in terms of increased efficiency, customer loyalty, and long-term profitability – are well worth the effort.

IKEA

IKEA, the Swedish multinational furniture retailer, is a prime example of a company that has successfully embraced strategic tradeoffs to establish a unique market position and achieve global success.

Founded in 1943 by Ingvar Kamprad, IKEA's vision was to offer a wide range of well-designed, functional home furnishing products at prices so low that as many people as possible could afford them. To realize this vision, IKEA made several key tradeoffs that have defined its business model and set it apart from competitors.

1. **Self-Assembly and Flat Packing:** One of IKEA's most significant tradeoffs is its focus on self-assembly furniture. By designing products that can be flat-packed and assembled by customers, IKEA can reduce

shipping and storage costs, passing these savings on to the consumer. This tradeoff means that customers must invest time and effort in assembling their furniture, but in return, they enjoy lower prices and the flexibility to transport their purchases easily.

2. **Limited Product Customization:** IKEA offers a wide range of furniture and home accessories, but it limits customization options to maintain its low-cost position. Customers can choose from a variety of predetermined styles, colors, and sizes, but they cannot request bespoke modifications. This tradeoff allows IKEA to benefit from economies of scale in production and keeps its inventory management simple and efficient.

3. **In-Store Experience:** IKEA stores are designed to be large, self-service warehouses where customers can browse, select, and collect their chosen items. This tradeoff means that customers do not receive personalized sales assistance, but in return, they have the freedom to explore products at their own pace and make independent decisions. IKEA also uses its store layout strategically, guiding customers through a predetermined route that exposes them to the full range of products.

4. **Location and Delivery:** IKEA stores are typically located on the outskirts of cities, where real estate is less expensive. This tradeoff allows the company to maintain its low-cost position but means that customers must travel further to shop. IKEA mitigates this inconvenience by offering delivery services for a fee, allowing customers to choose between saving money or time.

5. **Product Lifecycle:** IKEA's product range is not static; the company regularly introduces new items and discontinues others based on sales performance and consumer trends. This tradeoff means that customers may not always find the same products they purchased previously, but it allows IKEA to maintain a fresh, relevant product offering and keeps inventory costs down.

By consistently making these tradeoffs, IKEA has established a clear, differentiated market position. Its low-cost, self-service model appeals to a broad customer base, including young families, students, and budget-conscious shoppers. IKEA's focus on design and functionality also sets it apart from other low-cost retailers, allowing it to attract a wider range of customers.

By making deliberate choices about what it will and will not do, IKEA has created a unique value proposition that resonates with customers around the world.

* * *

12

The Principle of Strategic Fit

In business strategy, the principle of strategic fit emphasizes the importance of creating a coherent and mutually reinforcing alignment between a company's internal activities and its external environment. However, the true essence of strategic fit lies not just in the alignment of individual activities, but in the complex interconnections and linkages among them.

At its core, strategic fit is about creating a tightly woven tapestry of activities that support and reinforce each other. Each activity, whether it's a process, a resource allocation decision, or a customer interaction, should be designed and executed in a way that enhances the effectiveness of other activities. When activities are interconnected in this way, they create a powerful and sustainable competitive advantage that is difficult for rivals to imitate.

Consider the example of Toyota's legendary production system. Toyota's success in the automotive industry can be attributed to the tight strategic fit among its various activities, from product design and supplier management to manufacturing and quality control. Each activity is carefully designed to support and reinforce the others, creating a system that is optimized for efficiency, quality, and continuous improvement.

For instance, Toyota's just-in-time inventory system, which minimizes waste and reduces costs, is closely linked to its supplier management practices. Toyota works closely with its suppliers to ensure that parts are delivered in the right quantities and at the right time, reducing the need for large inventories and enabling a smooth flow of production. This, in turn, supports Toyota's quality control practices, as defects can be quickly identified and corrected without disrupting the entire production process.

Similarly, Toyota's emphasis on continuous improvement, or kaizen, is deeply embedded in its human resource practices. Employees at all levels are encouraged to identify and solve problems, and their suggestions for improvement are quickly implemented and shared across the organization. This culture of continuous improvement reinforces Toyota's manufacturing processes, as employees are constantly looking for ways to eliminate waste, reduce defects, and improve efficiency.

The interconnectedness of Toyota's activities creates a strategic fit that is incredibly difficult for competitors to replicate. Rivals may be able to copy individual elements of Toyota's system, such as its just-in-time inventory approach or its employee suggestion program, but they would struggle to recreate the complex web of linkages and reinforcing relationships that make the system so effective.

Another example of the power of strategic fit can be found in Apple's ecosystem of products and services. Apple's success in the technology industry is built on a foundation of tightly integrated hardware, software, and services that work together seamlessly to create a superior user experience.

At the heart of Apple's strategic fit is its vertically integrated business model. By designing and controlling every aspect of its products, from the chips and sensors to the operating system and user interface, Apple is able to create a cohesive and optimized user experience that is difficult for rivals to match. This vertical integration also enables Apple to capture more value from each product sale, as it doesn't have to share profits with third-party component suppliers or software developers.

Apple's strategic fit extends beyond its product design and manufacturing activities. The company's retail stores, for example, are carefully designed to showcase Apple's products and provide a high-touch customer experience. Apple's store employees are trained to be knowledgeable and helpful, and they use Apple's own products and services to demonstrate their capabilities to customers. This creates a powerful feedback loop, as satisfied customers are more likely to purchase additional Apple products and services, further reinforcing the company's ecosystem.

Apple's ecosystem also includes a vast network of third-party developers who create apps and accessories that enhance the value of Apple's products. By providing developers with a stable and well-documented platform, along with a large and loyal customer base, Apple has created a vibrant ecosystem that reinforces its competitive advantage. Customers are more likely to stick with Apple's products because they have access to a wide range of high-quality apps and accessories, while developers are more likely to prioritize Apple's platform because of its large and engaged user base.

The strategic fit among Apple's activities creates a virtuous cycle of value creation and capture that is incredibly difficult for competitors to disrupt. Rivals may be able to copy individual elements of Apple's ecosystem, such as its app store or its retail store design, but they would struggle to replicate the complex web of linkages and reinforcing relationships that make the ecosystem so powerful.

The principle of strategic fit has important implications for business leaders. To create a sustainable competitive advantage, leaders must look beyond individual activities and consider how they fit together as a coherent whole. This requires a deep understanding of the company's strengths, capabilities, and market position, as well as a willingness to make tough choices and trade-offs.

One of the key challenges in achieving strategic fit is the temptation to pursue multiple, conflicting objectives simultaneously. For example, a company may try to be both the low-cost provider and the premium brand in its industry, or it may try to serve both mass-market and niche customers with the same product line. These conflicting objectives can pull the company in different directions, diluting its focus and undermining its strategic fit.

To avoid this trap, leaders must be willing to make clear choices about where to compete and how to win. This may require divesting non-core businesses, exiting unprofitable markets, or foregoing certain opportunities that don't align with the company's strategy. It may also require investing heavily in certain activities or capabilities that are critical to the company's success, even if they don't generate immediate returns.

Another challenge in achieving strategic fit is the need to continuously adapt and evolve as market conditions change. While the underlying principles of strategic fit may remain constant, the specific activities and linkages that create competitive advantage may need to shift over time. Leaders must be attuned to changes in customer needs, competitive dynamics, and technological trends, and be willing to reconfigure their activities and linkages as needed.

Ultimately, by designing and executing activities in a way that supports and reinforces each other, companies can create a tightly woven tapestry that is difficult for rivals to unravel or replicate. This requires a deep understanding of the company's strengths and capabilities, as well as a willingness to make tough choices and trade-offs in pursuit of a coherent and mutually reinforcing strategy.

Southwest Airlines

Southwest Airlines is a prime example of a company that has achieved remarkable success through strategic fit among its various activities. The company's business model is built on a foundation of interlocking and mutually reinforcing activities that create a powerful and sustainable competitive advantage.

At the heart of Southwest's strategic fit is its unwavering focus on low costs and operational efficiency. This focus permeates every aspect of the company's operations, from its choice of aircraft to its hiring and training practices to its customer service philosophy.

One of the key activities that supports Southwest's low-cost strategy is its use of a standardized fleet of Boeing 737 aircraft. By operating a single type of aircraft, Southwest is able to simplify its maintenance and training operations, reduce spare parts inventories, and negotiate better deals with suppliers. This standardization also allows Southwest to achieve higher aircraft utilization rates, as pilots and crew can easily switch between planes without additional training.

Another critical activity that supports Southwest's low-cost strategy is its point-to-point route network. Unlike most major airlines, which operate hub-and-spoke networks that require passengers to connect through central hubs, Southwest flies direct routes between cities. This approach reduces the complexity of Southwest's operations, minimizes the time that aircraft spend on the ground, and allows for faster turnaround times between flights. It also enables Southwest to serve smaller, secondary airports that are often less congested and less expensive to operate in than major hubs.

Southwest's low-cost strategy is further reinforced by its no-frills approach to customer service. The company doesn't offer first-class seating, assigned seats, or in-flight meals, focusing instead on getting passengers to their destinations safely and efficiently. This approach not only reduces costs but also aligns with Southwest's egalitarian culture and its emphasis on simplicity and transparency.

Southwest's strategic fit extends beyond its operational activities to encompass its human resource practices as well. The company is known for its highly selective hiring process, which prioritizes cultural fit and attitude over specific job skills. Once hired, employees are given extensive training and empowered to make decisions that benefit customers. This approach creates a strong sense of loyalty and engagement among employees, which translates into better customer service and higher productivity.

Southwest's activities are also carefully designed to reinforce each other. For example, the company's use of a standardized fleet of aircraft not only reduces costs but also simplifies maintenance and training, which in turn supports its high aircraft utilization rates and its ability to offer frequent, reliable service. Similarly, Southwest's point-to-point route network not only reduces costs but also enables faster turnaround times and supports its high-frequency scheduling.

The interlocking nature of Southwest's activities creates a strategic fit that is very difficult for competitors to replicate. Rivals may be able to copy individual elements of Southwest's model, such as its use of a standardized fleet or its no-frills approach to customer service, but they would struggle to recreate the complex web of relationships and trade-offs that make the model so effective.

For example, a competitor that tried to copy Southwest's point-to-point route network would need to make significant investments in new aircraft, crew training, and airport facilities. They would also need to fundamentally rethink their pricing and revenue management strategies, as well as their relationships with travel agents and corporate customers. Even then, they would likely struggle to match Southwest's low costs and high efficiency, as they would lack the deep institutional knowledge and cultural alignment that Southwest has built over decades.

The strategic fit among Southwest's activities has allowed the company to consistently outperform its rivals in terms of profitability, growth, and customer satisfaction. Despite facing numerous challenges over the years, including recessions, fuel price spikes, and intense competition, Southwest has remained profitable for 47 consecutive years, a remarkable feat in the highly cyclical and capital-intensive airline industry.

Southwest's success demonstrates the power of strategic fit in creating a sustainable competitive advantage. By designing and executing a set of interlocking and mutually reinforcing activities that support its low-cost, high-efficiency strategy, Southwest has been able to build a business model that is both highly effective and very difficult for rivals to copy.

* * *

13

The Principle of Key Resources

In business strategy, the Principle of Key Resources stands as a vital pillar, guiding companies to identify, develop, and leverage the critical assets that underpin their competitive advantage and drive sustainable success. This principle recognizes that not all resources are created equal, and that focusing on the most strategic and valuable ones is essential to building a resilient, adaptable, and growth-oriented organization.

At its core, the Principle of Key Resources is about understanding what truly sets a company apart. In any given industry, competitors may have access to similar raw materials, technologies, or market opportunities. What distinguishes the winners from the rest is their ability to identify and cultivate the unique combination of resources that enables them to deliver superior value to customers, innovate faster than rivals, and adapt to changing market conditions.

Key resources can take many forms, depending on the nature of the business and its competitive environment. They may include tangible assets such as state-of-the-art equipment, proprietary technologies, or prime real estate locations. They may also encompass intangible assets like brand reputation, intellectual property, unique company culture, or deep customer relationships. The most powerful key resources are often those that are rare, difficult to imitate, and strategically valuable, as they provide a durable source of competitive advantage.

To identify their key resources, companies must engage in a rigorous process of self-reflection and analysis. This involves looking beyond the obvious and digging deep into the core of the business to uncover the true drivers of value creation. It requires a keen understanding of the company's strengths and weaknesses, as well as the evolving needs and preferences of its customers. By asking tough questions and challenging assumptions, companies can surface insights into the resources that truly differentiate them and enable them to achieve their strategic objectives.

Once key resources are identified, the focus shifts to developing and leveraging them for maximum impact. This is where the Principle of Key Resources intersects with other critical aspects of business strategy, such as innovation, customer segmentation, and organizational design. By aligning key resources with the company's value proposition, target customers, and core capabilities, leaders can create a powerful, mutually reinforcing system that drives superior performance.

For example, a company that identifies its proprietary technology as a key resource might invest heavily in research and development to maintain its edge, while also tailoring its marketing and sales efforts to highlight the unique benefits of its technology to target customers. A company that recognizes its talent as a key resource might focus on attracting, developing, and retaining the best people, while also designing its organizational structure and culture to foster collaboration, creativity, and continuous learning.

Leveraging key resources also requires a keen understanding of the external environment and the ability to adapt to changing circumstances. In today's fast-paced, unpredictable business landscape, even the most valuable resources can become obsolete or commoditized over time. To stay ahead, companies must continuously monitor their key resources, invest in their development, and seek out new ways to deploy them for competitive advantage.

This is where the concept of dynamic capabilities comes into play. Dynamic capabilities refer to a company's ability to sense and seize new opportunities, reconfigure its resources and processes, and adapt to changing market conditions. By cultivating dynamic capabilities, companies can more effectively leverage their key resources in the face of disruption, uncertainty, and complexity. This might involve rapidly reallocating resources to new growth areas, forming strategic partnerships to access complementary assets, or experimenting with new business models to unlock untapped value.

However, the Principle of Key Resources is not without its challenges. One common pitfall is the temptation to spread resources too thin, trying to be everything to everyone. This can lead to a lack of focus, diluted value proposition, and mediocre performance across the board. To avoid this trap, companies must be disciplined in their resource allocation, prioritizing the areas that offer the greatest strategic value and saying no to opportunities that don't align with their core strengths.

Another challenge is the risk of becoming overly reliant on a single key resource, leaving the company vulnerable to disruption or competitive threats. To mitigate this risk, companies must actively seek to diversify their resource base, developing multiple sources of competitive advantage that can provide resilience and flexibility in the face of change. This might involve investing in complementary assets, building a portfolio of strategic partnerships, or exploring adjacent market opportunities.

In conclusion, by identifying, developing, and leveraging the unique assets that set them apart, companies can create a powerful source of competitive advantage that enables them to outperform rivals, adapt to change, and create lasting value for customers and stakeholders alike. While the journey is not always easy, the rewards of a focused, resource-driven strategy are well worth the effort. As such, the Principle of Key Resources should be a top priority for any leader seeking to build a truly great and enduring organization.

Novo Nordisk

Novo Nordisk is a Danish pharmaceutical company that specializes in diabetes care. Their key resources include:

1. **Patent-protected insulin formulations:** Novo Nordisk has developed

a range of innovative insulin products protected by patents, including long-acting and fast-acting insulin analogs. These proprietary formulations are a critical resource that underpins their competitive position in diabetes care.

2. **Deep expertise in protein engineering:** Over decades, Novo Nordisk has cultivated world-leading capabilities in engineering insulin and other therapeutic proteins. This accumulated knowledge and skill in manipulating protein structures to optimize drug performance is a unique and valuable resource.
3. **Global manufacturing and supply chain:** Novo Nordisk has established a vast network of high-tech production facilities and distribution channels to ensure reliable, high-quality supply of their diabetes medicines worldwide. This manufacturing and supply chain infrastructure is a key resource for serving their global customer base.
4. **Relationships with healthcare providers:** Novo Nordisk has built strong, long-term relationships with physicians, nurses, and diabetes educators around the world. These deep connections with front-line healthcare professionals is a valuable resource for understanding evolving patient needs, providing education, and ultimately delivering better diabetes care.

These are the unique, valuable, and hard-to-imitate assets that Novo Nordisk has developed over time. They form the foundation of the company's competitive advantage in the diabetes care market.

Zara

Zara, founded in 1975, has grown to become one of the world's largest fashion retailers, with over 2,200 stores in 96 countries. The company's success can be attributed to its unique business model, which is built on a foundation of key resources, core competencies and strategic activities that enable it to respond quickly to changing fashion trends and customer preferences.

Key Resources:

1. **Vertically integrated supply chain:** Zara's agile and responsive supply chain is a critical resource that allows the company to quickly design, produce, and distribute new fashion styles. The company's ownership of its production facilities and tight control over its supply chain enable it to maintain strict quality standards and respond rapidly to changing market demands.
2. **In-house design team:** Zara's team of over 700 talented designers is a key resource that drives the company's ability to create new styles based on the latest fashion trends and customer preferences. This in-house design capability allows Zara to continuously introduce new products and stay ahead of the competition.
3. **Prime store locations:** Zara's carefully selected store locations in high-traffic areas are a valuable resource that contributes to the company's success. These prime locations help attract customers, increase brand visibility, and drive sales.
4. **Advanced information technology systems:** Zara's investments in advanced IT systems, including point-of-sale systems, inventory management tools, and data analytics platforms, are a key resource that enables the company to collect and analyze real-time data from its stores. This information helps Zara make informed decisions about production, distribution, and merchandising.
5. **Skilled and experienced workforce:** Zara's talented and experienced employees, including designers, store managers, and supply chain professionals, are a vital human resource. Their skills, knowledge, and dedication contribute to the company's ability to execute its strategic activities effectively.

These key resources, along with Zara's core competencies and strategic activities, form a powerful and mutually reinforcing system that drives the company's competitive advantage in the fast-fashion industry. By continually investing in and leveraging these resources, Zara has been able to establish itself as a global leader and maintain its position at the forefront of fashion retail.

* * *

14

The Principle of Key Partners

In today's interconnected business world, no company can succeed entirely on its own. Even the most successful businesses rely on a network of key partners to help them achieve their strategic objectives. These partners can include suppliers, distributors, collaborators, and even competitors in some cases. The Principle of Key Partners recognizes that building and maintaining strong relationships with these critical stakeholders is essential for long-term business success.

One of the primary reasons why key partners are so important is that they can provide access to resources and capabilities that a company may not have in-house. For example, a manufacturer may partner with a supplier that has expertise in a particular type of raw material or component. By leveraging this partner's knowledge and experience, the manufacturer can improve the quality of its products and reduce costs. Similarly, a company may partner with a distributor that has established relationships with key customers or a strong presence in a particular market. By working with this partner, the company can expand its reach and grow its business more quickly than it could on its own.

Another key benefit of partnerships is that they can help companies to share risk and reduce uncertainty. When a company enters a new market or launches a new product, there are always risks involved. By partnering with another company that has experience in that market or with that type of product, a company can mitigate some of these risks and increase its chances of success. Partnerships can also provide a way for companies to pool resources and share the costs of expensive projects or initiatives.

Of course, not all partnerships are created equal. To truly leverage the Principle of Key Partners, companies need to be strategic in how they choose and manage their relationships. This starts with identifying the right partners in the first place. Companies should look for partners that share their values and have complementary strengths and capabilities. They should also consider the long-term potential of the partnership and whether there is a clear alignment of interests.

Once a partnership is established, it's important to invest time and resources into maintaining and strengthening the relationship. This may involve regular communication, joint planning sessions, and even co-location of teams. It's also important to have clear expectations and governance structures in place to ensure that both parties are held accountable and that the partnership stays on track.

One company that has successfully leveraged the Principle of Key Partners is Apple. From its earliest days, Apple has relied on a network of key partners to help it bring its innovative products to market. For example, the company has long-standing relationships with suppliers like Foxconn and Samsung, which manufacture many of its key components. Apple has also partnered with carriers like AT&T and Verizon to distribute its products and with developers to create a thriving ecosystem of apps and services. By carefully choosing and nurturing these partnerships, Apple has been able to focus on what it does best – designing and marketing iconic products – while still maintaining control over the end-to-end customer experience.

In conclusion, by building strong relationships with suppliers, distributors, collaborators, and other key stakeholders, companies can access new resources and capabilities, share risk and uncertainty, and ultimately achieve their strategic objectives more quickly and effectively. Of course, partnerships are not a panacea and require careful management and attention to detail. But when done right, they can be a powerful tool for driving growth, innovation, and long-term success.

STRATEGY IKIGAI

* * *

15

The Principle of Customer Relationships

In business strategy, the Principle of Customer Relationships stands as a critical pillar, guiding companies to forge strong, lasting connections with their customers. This principle recognizes that the success of any business hinges on its ability to understand, satisfy, and exceed customer expectations. By fostering meaningful relationships, companies can create a loyal customer base, enhance brand reputation, and drive sustainable growth.

At the core of the Principle of Customer Relationships lies the understanding that customers are not mere transactions but individuals with unique needs, desires, and emotions. To build successful relationships, companies must first invest in understanding their customers deeply. This involves gathering insights through market research, customer feedback, and data analysis. By gaining a comprehensive view of customer preferences, pain points, and behaviors, companies can tailor their products, services, and communication to resonate with their target audience. By considering what kind of customer relationships each segment needs, businesses can ensure that their strategy design and plans align with the needs and preferences of their target audience. This information can guide resource allocation, marketing efforts, and product development.

Once a deep understanding of customers is established, the focus shifts to creating experiences that cater to the specific needs of each customer segment. While some segments may value personalized interactions, others may prioritize factors such as efficiency, convenience, or cost-effectiveness. Companies that excel in customer relationships recognize these differences and adapt their approach accordingly. For segments that value personalization, this can manifest in customized product recommendations, tailored service options, or targeted marketing messages. By making these customers feel valued and understood, companies can differentiate themselves and foster a sense of loyalty. Understanding customer relationships allows businesses to develop targeted strategies for different customer segments. For example, a company may create a loyalty program for high-value customers or develop a specific communication plan for new customers to foster strong relationships from the start.

Effective communication is another crucial aspect of building strong customer relationships. Companies must establish clear, consistent, and responsive communication to engage with customers at every touchpoint. This includes proactive outreach to keep customers informed about new offerings, updates, or changes. It also involves active listening and promptly addressing customer inquiries, concerns, or complaints. By being accessible and responsive, companies demonstrate their commitment to customer satisfaction and build trust. Customer relationships also inform us about communication channels through which we need to approach customers, which would help us to plan everything including resources, skills, capabilities, and so on, ensuring that they all form a coherent chain with all activities and strategy.

In today's digital age, technology plays a pivotal role in nurturing customer relationships. Companies must leverage digital platforms, such as social media, mobile apps, and customer portals, to create seamless and convenient experiences. These platforms provide opportunities for real-time interaction, personalized content delivery, and self-service options. By harnessing the power of technology, companies can enhance customer engagement, gather valuable feedback, and streamline customer support processes.

However, building customer relationships goes beyond transactional interactions. Companies must also focus on creating emotional connections and shared values. This involves aligning the brand's purpose and values with those of the customers. By supporting causes that matter to their customers, engaging in corporate social responsibility initiatives, and demonstrating a genuine commitment to making a positive impact, companies can forge deeper emotional bonds. When customers feel a strong affinity with a brand's values, they are more likely to become loyal advocates and long-term partners.

Measuring and monitoring the health of customer relationships is essential for continuous improvement. Companies should establish key performance indicators (KPIs) to track customer satisfaction, loyalty, and lifetime value. Regular surveys, feedback mechanisms, and customer analytics provide valuable insights into the strength of relationships. By actively listening to customer feedback and acting upon it, companies can identify areas for improvement, address pain points, and adapt their strategies to meet evolving customer needs. Incorporating customer relationship considerations into the strategy design process allows businesses to set clear goals and metrics related to customer satisfaction, retention, and loyalty. These goals can be used to measure the success of the strategy and make data-driven decisions for improvement.

By considering customer relationships during the planning stage, businesses can estimate the potential lifetime value of different customer segments. This insight can inform decisions about customer acquisition, retention, and resource allocation. By understanding the importance of customer relationships, businesses can allocate resources more effectively. This may involve investing in customer relationship management (CRM) systems, training employees in customer service best practices, or dedicating resources to customer feedback analysis.

Ultimately, the Principle of Customer Relationships emphasizes that building strong, mutually beneficial connections with customers is not a one-time effort but an ongoing commitment. It requires a customer-centric mindset, empathy, and a willingness to continuously adapt and improve. By prioritizing customer relationships as a strategic imperative, companies can create a sustainable competitive advantage, foster brand loyalty, and drive long-term success in the ever-changing business landscape.

Zappos

Zappos has built its brand and business strategy around delivering exceptional customer service and fostering strong customer relationships. From its early days, Zappos recognized that customer loyalty and word-of-mouth referrals were essential for long-term success in the highly competitive e-commerce industry.

One of the key ways Zappos builds strong customer relationships is through its commitment to personalized service. The company empowers its customer service representatives to go above and beyond to satisfy customers. They are encouraged to spend as much time as needed on the phone with customers, build personal connections, and find creative solutions to their needs. This level of personalized attention makes customers feel valued and appreciated, leading to high levels of customer satisfaction and loyalty.

Zappos also leverages technology to enhance customer relationships. The company offers a user-friendly website, easy navigation, and a simple return process. It provides detailed product information, customer reviews, and size recommendations to help customers make informed decisions. Zappos also offers free shipping and returns, eliminating any risk or inconvenience for customers.

In addition to personalized service and seamless digital experiences, Zappos invests in building emotional connections with customers. The company is known for its unique corporate culture, which emphasizes happiness, positivity, and a fun work environment. This culture translates into the interactions customers have with Zappos employees, creating a memorable and enjoyable experience.

Zappos also demonstrates its commitment to customer relationships through its "Zappos Insights" program. This initiative offers tours of the company's headquarters, workshops, and training sessions to share its customer-centric philosophy with other businesses. By openly sharing its strategies and best practices, Zappos reinforces its dedication to helping others build strong customer relationships.

The results of Zappos' focus on customer relationships are evident in its success. The company has consistently achieved high customer satisfaction ratings, with a significant portion of its sales coming from repeat customers and referrals. Zappos has also been recognized with numerous awards for its outstanding customer service and company culture.

* * *

16

The Principle of Communication Channels

In today's interconnected world, the way businesses communicate with their customers, partners, and stakeholders has become a critical factor in crafting a successful strategy. The Principle of Communication Channels emphasizes the importance of selecting, managing, and optimizing the various channels through which a company interacts with its audience. By strategically leveraging different communication channels, businesses can effectively reach their target market, build strong relationships, and achieve their strategic goals.

Understanding the communication landscape is the first step in applying the Principle of Communication Channels. The modern business landscape offers a wide array of communication channels, each with its own strengths, limitations, and audience preferences. To make informed decisions about resource allocation, businesses must assess the reach, engagement potential, and cost-effectiveness of each channel. Aligning the channel strategy with the preferences and behaviors of the target audience is crucial for maximizing the impact of communication efforts. Different customer segments may have distinct preferences based on factors such as age, lifestyle, and technological savvy.

Integrating communication channels into the initial strategy design and planning process is essential for building a successful business strategy. By considering communication channels early on, businesses can ensure that their overall strategy is cohesive and aligned with their target audience's preferences. This proactive approach helps in identifying the most effective channels for reaching and engaging with customers, allowing businesses to allocate resources accordingly. Moreover, incorporating communication channels into the planning stage enables businesses to set clear objectives, define key performance indicators (KPIs), and establish a framework for measuring the success of their communication efforts.

Developing an integrated channel strategy is another key aspect of the Principle of Communication Channels. Instead of treating each channel as a standalone entity, businesses should strive to create a seamless communication experience across all touchpoints. Consistency in messaging, branding, and tone across different channels reinforces brand identity, builds trust, and creates a unified customer experience. An integrated approach allows businesses to leverage the strengths of each channel and create synergies that amplify the overall impact of their communication efforts.

To continuously improve the effectiveness of their communication channels, businesses must adopt a data-driven approach. Collecting and analyzing data on channel performance, customer engagement, and conversion rates provides valuable insights into what works and what doesn't. This data-driven optimization enables businesses to make informed decisions about resource allocation, content optimization, and channel prioritization. Regular monitoring and adjustment of the channel strategy based on data-driven insights are essential for staying relevant and effective in the face of changing consumer behaviors and expectations.

Adapting to the evolving communication channel landscape is crucial for businesses to stay competitive. New platforms and technologies emerge regularly, and businesses must be prepared to experiment with emerging channels to reach audiences in innovative ways. This requires a willingness to learn, test, and refine the communication approach continuously. However, businesses must also strike a balance in their channel mix to avoid spreading resources too thin. Prioritizing channels that align best with the target audience, strategic goals, and available resources is key to achieving optimal results.

Measuring and refining channel performance is an ongoing process in the Principle of Communication Channels. Establishing clear metrics and KPIs for each channel allows businesses to track the effectiveness of their communication efforts. Regular analysis of reach, engagement, conversion rates, customer satisfaction, and return on investment helps identify areas for improvement and enables data-driven decision-making. Continuous measurement and refinement keep businesses agile and responsive to changing audience preferences and market dynamics.

Fostering two-way communication is another essential aspect of the Principle of Communication Channels. Businesses should create opportunities for dialogue and engagement with customers and stakeholders. Leveraging social media platforms to respond to inquiries and feedback, conducting surveys to gather insights, and creating interactive content encourages audience participation. Actively listening and responding to customer voices across different channels demonstrates a commitment to customer satisfaction and helps build stronger relationships.

To effectively implement the Principle of Communication Channels, businesses must invest in employee training and alignment. All employees who interact with customers or contribute to communication efforts should be well-versed in the company's channel strategy, brand guidelines, and communication best practices. Regular training ensures consistency in messaging and tone across all touchpoints and helps employees adapt to evolving channel trends and customer preferences.

In conclusion, the Principle of Communication Channels is a critical component of building a successful business strategy. By understanding the communication landscape, aligning channels with customer preferences, developing an integrated channel strategy, and continuously optimizing based on data-driven insights, businesses can create impactful and engaging communication experiences. Incorporating communication channels into the initial strategy design and planning process ensures cohesion and alignment with overall business objectives.

Apple

Let's take a look at how Apple, a global technology giant, applies the Principle of Communication Channels in its business strategy.

1. **Integrating Communication Channels into Strategy Design:** Apple carefully considers communication channels when designing its overall business strategy. The company recognizes the importance of reaching customers through various touchpoints and aligns its channel strategy with its target audience's preferences. Apple's strategy involves a mix of online and offline channels, including its website, Apple Stores, social media, and targeted advertising, to effectively communicate with its customers.
2. **Consistent Brand Experience Across Channels:** Apple is known for its consistent brand experience across all communication channels. Whether a customer visits an Apple Store, browses the website, or interacts with the company on social media, they encounter the same sleek design, intuitive user experience, and high-quality content. This consistency reinforces Apple's brand identity, builds trust, and creates a seamless customer journey.
3. **Leveraging Digital Channels:** Apple effectively leverages digital channels to reach and engage with its target audience. The company's website serves as a central hub for product information, tutorials, and customer support. Apple also has a strong presence on social media platforms like Twitter, Instagram, and YouTube, where it shares product updates, engaging content, and interacts with customers. These digital channels allow Apple to connect with its tech-savvy audience and foster brand loyalty.
4. **Experiential Retail Stores:** Apple's retail stores serve as a powerful communication channel, providing customers with an immersive and experiential brand encounter. The stores feature sleek designs, hands-on product demonstrations, and knowledgeable staff who guide customers through Apple's ecosystem. These stores not only showcase Apple's

products but also serve as a platform for customer education, support, and community building.

5. **Targeted Advertising:** Apple employs targeted advertising to reach specific customer segments with relevant messages. The company uses data-driven insights to understand customer preferences and delivers personalized ads across various channels, including online platforms, billboards, and television commercials. By tailoring its advertising to specific audience segments, Apple effectively communicates the benefits of its products and drives customer engagement.

6. **Events and Keynotes:** Apple's special events and keynotes serve as powerful communication channels to generate buzz, introduce new products, and engage with its global audience. These highly anticipated events, such as the annual Apple Worldwide Developers Conference (WWDC) and iPhone launches, are streamed live across multiple platforms, reaching millions of viewers worldwide. These events not only showcase Apple's innovations but also reinforce its brand image and leadership in the technology industry.

7. **Customer Support and Feedback Channels:** Apple provides multiple channels for customer support and feedback, including its website, phone support, and in-store Genius Bar. These channels allow customers to seek assistance, resolve issues, and provide valuable feedback. Apple's focus on customer support and its ability to address concerns through various channels contribute to high customer satisfaction and brand loyalty.

8. **Continuous Optimization and Adaptation:** Apple continuously monitors and analyzes the performance of its communication channels to optimize its strategy. The company uses data-driven insights to understand customer preferences, measure the effectiveness of its campaigns, and make informed decisions about resource allocation. Apple also stays attuned to emerging channels and technologies, such as voice assistants and augmented reality, to explore new ways of engaging with its audience.

By integrating communication channels into its strategy design, maintaining a consistent brand experience, leveraging digital platforms, creating experiential retail stores, employing targeted advertising, hosting iconic events, providing robust customer support, and continuously optimizing its approach, Apple exemplifies the effective application of the Principle of Communication Channels in building a successful business strategy.

* * *

17

The Principle of Big Picture

In the fast-paced and ever-changing business world, it is easy for leaders to get caught up in the day-to-day operations and short-term challenges of running a company. However, successful business strategy requires a broader perspective—one that takes into account the complex interplay of internal and external factors that shape an organization's future. This is where the Principle of Big Picture comes into play.

The Principle of Big Picture is about understanding the larger context in which a business operates and making strategic decisions that are informed by this understanding. It involves looking beyond the immediate horizon and considering the long-term implications of choices made in the present. By adopting a big-picture mindset, business leaders can anticipate future trends, identify potential risks and opportunities, and make proactive decisions that position their organizations for sustained success.

One of the key aspects of the Principle of Big Picture is environmental scanning. This involves continuously monitoring and analyzing the various factors that influence a business, such as economic conditions, technological advancements, social and demographic shifts, political and regulatory changes, and competitive dynamics. By staying attuned to these external forces, companies can adapt their strategies to capitalize on emerging opportunities and mitigate potential threats.

For example, consider the rise of digital technologies and the internet. Companies that recognized the transformative potential of these developments early on and adapted their strategies accordingly—such as Amazon, Netflix, and Apple—have been able to create entirely new markets and disrupt traditional industries. On the other hand, companies that failed to see the big picture and clung to outdated business models—such as Blockbuster and Kodak—have struggled to remain relevant in the face of digital disruption.

Another important aspect of the Principle of Big Picture is systems thinking. This involves recognizing that businesses are complex systems made up of interconnected and interdependent parts. Changes in one area of the business can have ripple effects throughout the entire organization, and even beyond its boundaries. By taking a systems view, leaders can better understand the relationships between different elements of their business and make more holistic and integrated decisions.

For instance, a company's decision to outsource certain functions may have immediate cost-saving benefits, but it could also have long-term implications for quality control, intellectual property protection, and customer satisfaction. Similarly, a company's choice of suppliers can have far-reaching consequences for its reputation, as well as its social and environmental impact. By considering these broader systemic effects, companies can make more responsible and sustainable choices.

The Principle of Big Picture also requires a focus on long-term value creation rather than short-term gains. This means making investments and strategic decisions that may not pay off immediately but are essential for the company's long-term success. It involves balancing the needs of different stakeholders—including shareholders, employees, customers, and communities—and making choices that create shared value over time.

For example, a company may choose to invest heavily in research and development, even if it means sacrificing short-term profits, because it believes that innovation is critical to its long-term competitiveness. Similarly, a company may decide to prioritize environmental sustainability and social responsibility, even if it requires upfront costs because it recognizes that these factors are increasingly important to customers, investors, and society as a whole.

To effectively apply the Principle of Big Picture, business leaders need to cultivate a strategic mindset and develop the skills and tools to analyze complex systems and make informed decisions. This may involve:

1. Engaging in scenario planning and strategic foresight to anticipate future trends and possibilities.
2. Building diverse teams and encouraging cross-functional collaboration to promote systems thinking and innovation.
3. Investing in data analytics and business intelligence to gain insights into customer behavior, market dynamics, and organizational performance.
4. Developing a clear and compelling vision for the future of the organization and communicating it effectively to all stakeholders.
5. Cultivating a culture of learning and adaptability that enables the organization to respond quickly to changing circumstances.

Ultimately, the Principle of Big Picture is about taking a strategic, long-term view of the business and making decisions that are informed by a deep understanding of the larger context in which it operates. By embracing this principle, companies can position themselves for sustainable growth and success in an increasingly complex and dynamic business environment.

However, it is important to note that the Principle of Big Picture should not be pursued in isolation from the other key principles of successful business strategy. Vision, core values, customer centricity, value proposition, focus, differentiation, core competencies, strategic activities, tradeoffs, and strategic fit are all essential elements of a comprehensive and effective strategy.

The challenge for business leaders is to balance these different principles and find the right mix that works for their specific organization and context. This requires ongoing reflection, analysis, and adaptation as the business environment evolves and new challenges and opportunities arise.

In conclusion, the Principle of Big Picture is a crucial component of successful business strategy in today's complex and rapidly changing world.

By maintaining a holistic view of the organization and its environment, making informed and proactive decisions, and focusing on long-term value creation, companies can position themselves for sustained growth and success. As business leaders navigate the challenges and opportunities of the 21st century, the ability to see the big picture will be an increasingly important strategic advantage.

Jeff Bezos

One prominent example of a leader who exemplified the Principle of Big Picture is Jeff Bezos, the founder and former CEO of Amazon. From the company's inception, Bezos had a clear and ambitious vision for Amazon's future, which extended far beyond its initial focus on online book sales.

Bezos recognized early on the immense potential of the internet and e-commerce to transform the way people shop and consume goods and services. He saw the big picture of how technology could be leveraged to create a seamless and personalized customer experience, and he made strategic decisions that positioned Amazon to capitalize on this opportunity.

For instance, Bezos invested heavily in building a robust technological infrastructure and logistics network that could support the company's rapid growth and expansion into new markets and product categories. He also prioritized customer-centricity and innovation, constantly seeking new ways to add value and improve the customer experience.

Bezos' big-picture thinking was evident in his famous "Day 1" philosophy, which emphasized the importance of maintaining a startup mentality and focusing on long-term value creation rather than short-term profits. He encouraged his team to think like owners and to make bold bets on the future, even if it meant sacrificing short-term gains.

Under Bezos' leadership, Amazon expanded far beyond its initial focus on books to become a global leader in e-commerce, cloud computing, artificial intelligence, and other cutting-edge technologies. The company has disrupted multiple industries and created entirely new markets, cementing its position as one of the most valuable and influential companies in the world.

Bezos' ability to see the big picture and make proactive, long-term strategic decisions has been a key factor in Amazon's success. His leadership style and strategic vision have become a model for other business leaders looking to build enduring and impactful companies.

Lou Gerstner

Lou Gerstner, former CEO of IBM, is another excellent example of a leader who embodied the Principle of Big Picture in his approach to transforming the company. When Gerstner took over as CEO in 1993, IBM was on the brink of collapse, with declining revenues, mounting losses, and a lack of clear strategic direction.

Gerstner recognized that IBM's problems were not just financial, but strategic and cultural as well. He saw the big picture of how the technology industry was evolving and realized that IBM needed to fundamentally reinvent itself to remain relevant and competitive.

One of Gerstner's first moves was to shift IBM's focus from hardware to software and services. He recognized that the future of the industry was in providing integrated solutions and consulting services to help customers leverage technology to transform their businesses. This required a significant shift in IBM's business model and organizational structure.

Gerstner also saw the importance of building a more customer-centric and collaborative culture within IBM. He broke down internal silos and encouraged cross-functional teamwork and innovation. He emphasized the importance of listening to customers and understanding their needs, rather than just pushing products.

Another key aspect of Gerstner's big-picture approach was his focus on globalization. He recognized that IBM needed to be a truly global company, with a presence in key markets around the world. He invested in building a global infrastructure and workforce, and he encouraged a culture of diversity and inclusion.

Gerstner's big-picture thinking also extended to IBM's brand and reputation. He saw the value in positioning IBM as a trusted partner and thought leader in the industry. He invested in marketing and communications to build the IBM brand and to showcase the company's expertise and innovations.

Under Gerstner's leadership, IBM underwent a dramatic transformation. The company shifted its focus to high-value services and solutions, such as IT consulting, systems integration, and e-business. It became a leader in emerging technologies such as the internet, e-commerce, and mobile computing. And it regained its position as one of the most respected and influential companies in the world.

Gerstner's success at IBM illustrates the power of the Principle of Big Picture in driving strategic change and organizational transformation. By taking a holistic, long-term view of the company and its environment, and by making bold and proactive decisions, Gerstner was able to turn around a struggling giant and position it for success in the 21st century.

* * *

18

The Principle of Attention to Detail (Thinking Small)

In the pursuit of grand visions and ambitious strategies, it is easy for business leaders to overlook the smaller, more mundane aspects of running a company. However, the Principle of Attention to Detail suggests that these seemingly minor factors can have a significant impact on a business's overall success. By "thinking small" and focusing on the finer points of execution, companies can create a strong foundation for their broader strategic goals.

One of the primary areas where attention to detail is critical is in the realm of customer experience. In today's competitive business landscape, customers have more choices than ever before, and they are increasingly demanding seamless, personalized, and high-quality experiences from the brands they interact with. Companies that neglect the small details of the customer journey—from the usability of their website to the quality of their packaging and the responsiveness of their customer service—risk losing customers to competitors who are more attentive to these factors.

For example, consider the success of Apple, a company renowned for its obsessive attention to detail. From the sleek design of its products to the intuitive user interface of its software and the immersive experience of its retail stores, Apple has built a loyal customer base by consistently delivering on the small things that matter to users. This focus on detail extends to every aspect of the company's operations, from the precision of its supply chain management to the quality of its customer support.

Another area where attention to detail is essential is in the execution of a company's strategic initiatives. While it is important to have a clear vision and direction for the business, the success of any strategy ultimately depends on how well it is implemented on the ground. This requires a focus on the operational details, such as resource allocation, process optimization, and performance monitoring.

One company that exemplifies this principle is Toyota, which has long been admired for its lean manufacturing practices and continuous improvement philosophy. Toyota's success is built on a relentless attention to detail, from the standardization of its production processes to the empowerment of its frontline workers to identify and solve problems in real-time. By continuously refining and optimizing its operations, Toyota has been able to maintain a level of efficiency and quality that sets it apart from its competitors.

Attention to detail is also critical when it comes to financial management and risk mitigation. In the pursuit of growth and profitability, it can be tempting for companies to cut corners or overlook potential risks in their operations. However, this short-term thinking can lead to long-term problems, such as financial instability, legal liabilities, and reputational damage.

For instance, the 2008 financial crisis was largely caused by a lack of attention to detail in the lending practices of banks and other financial institutions. By neglecting to properly assess the creditworthiness of borrowers and the risks associated with complex financial instruments, these organizations set the stage for a global economic meltdown. In contrast, companies that maintain a disciplined approach to financial management and risk assessment are better positioned to weather economic downturns and emerge stronger on the other side.

Attention to detail is not just about avoiding negative outcomes, however. It is also about identifying and capitalizing on small opportunities that can add up to significant advantages over time. This requires a curious and proactive mindset, as well as a willingness to experiment and iterate based on feedback and data.

One company that has mastered this approach is Amazon, which has built its success on a constant focus on incremental improvements and customer-centric innovation. From its early days as an online bookseller to its current status as a global e-commerce and technology giant, Amazon has relentlessly pursued small enhancements to its business model and customer experience. Whether it's optimizing its warehouse operations, personalizing its product recommendations, or constantly refining its delivery options, Amazon's attention to detail has allowed it to stay ahead of the curve and drive incremental growth over time.

To effectively apply the Principle of Attention to Detail, business leaders need to cultivate a culture of excellence and continuous improvement within their organizations. This may involve:

1. Setting high standards for quality and performance across all aspects of the business, and holding teams accountable for meeting those standards.
2. Encouraging a data-driven approach to decision-making, using metrics and feedback loops to continuously monitor and optimize processes and outcomes.
3. Empowering frontline employees to identify and solve problems in real-time, and providing them with the tools and resources they need to do so effectively.
4. Fostering a culture of experimentation and learning, where small failures are seen as opportunities for growth and improvement rather than reasons for punishment.
5. Paying close attention to the needs and preferences of customers, and using those insights to drive incremental improvements and innovations in products, services, and experiences.

Ultimately, the Principle of Attention to Detail is about recognizing that success is often the result of many small, cumulative actions rather than a single grand gesture. By focusing on the finer points of execution and continuously refining and optimizing their operations, companies can build a strong foundation for sustainable growth and competitive advantage.

However, it is important to strike a balance between attention to detail and the ability to adapt and innovate in response to changing circumstances. While a focus on small improvements can drive incremental gains, companies also need to be able to step back and rethink their strategies when necessary. This requires a degree of flexibility and agility that can be challenging to maintain in large, complex organizations.

Moreover, attention to detail should not come at the expense of the big picture. Leaders need to be able to zoom in and out, focusing on the small details when necessary while also keeping an eye on the broader strategic context. This requires a keen sense of priorities and the ability to allocate resources and attention appropriately.

Steve Jobs and iPod

Steve Jobs, the co-founder and former CEO of Apple, was known for his obsessive attention to detail, particularly when it came to product design and user experience. One of the best examples of this is the development of the iPod, which revolutionized the music industry and set the stage for Apple's dominance in the mobile device market.

When Jobs and his team set out to create the iPod, they were entering a crowded market of digital music players. However, Jobs saw an opportunity to differentiate Apple's product through a relentless focus on simplicity, ease of use, and design elegance. He believed that by paying attention to every detail of the user experience, Apple could create a product that would stand out from the competition and capture the hearts and minds of consumers.

One of the key details that Jobs focused on was the iPod's user interface. He insisted on a simple, intuitive navigation system that would allow users to easily browse and select their music. The iPod's iconic click wheel design was a result of this focus on simplicity, as it allowed users to scroll through their music library and adjust volume with a single thumb motion. Jobs and his team went through countless iterations of the click wheel design, tweaking everything from the size and placement of the buttons to the tactile feedback of the wheel itself.

Another detail that Jobs paid close attention to was the iPod's industrial design. He wanted the device to be sleek, compact, and visually striking, with a minimalist aesthetic that would appeal to style-conscious consumers. To achieve this, Jobs and his team obsessed over every aspect of the iPod's form factor, from the materials used in its construction to the placement of its ports and buttons. They even went so far as to create custom manufacturing processes to achieve the desired level of precision and consistency in the iPod's enclosure.

Jobs also recognized the importance of seamless integration between hardware and software in creating a compelling user experience. He insisted that the iPod's software be designed from the ground up to work seamlessly with the device's hardware, creating a fluid and intuitive experience for users. This attention to detail extended to every aspect of the software, from the visual design of the user interface to the algorithms used for music playback and synchronization with iTunes.

Even the iPod's packaging was a subject of Jobs' obsessive attention to detail. He believed that the unboxing experience was a critical moment in the customer journey, and he wanted it to be as memorable and delightful as possible. To achieve this, Jobs and his team created packaging that was minimalist, elegant, and easy to open, with careful attention paid to every aspect of the materials, layout, and branding.

Beyond the product itself, Jobs also paid close attention to the details of the iPod's marketing and positioning. He recognized that the iPod was not just a technical achievement, but a cultural phenomenon that could transform the way people consumed and shared music. To capitalize on this opportunity, Jobs and his team created a series of iconic advertisements and marketing campaigns that emphasized the iPod's simplicity, style, and emotional appeal. They also formed strategic partnerships with music labels and artists to ensure that the iPod had a deep and diverse content library that would keep users engaged and loyal.

Ultimately, Jobs' attention to detail in the development and marketing of the iPod paid off handsomely for Apple. The device quickly became a cultural icon and a commercial blockbuster, selling over 400 million units worldwide and establishing Apple as a leader in the mobile device market. More importantly, the success of the iPod laid the groundwork for Apple's subsequent innovations, such as the iPhone and iPad, which have transformed entire industries and reshaped the way we live and work.

Ritz-Carlton Hotel Company

The Ritz-Carlton's success is built on a fundamental commitment to putting the guest first and anticipating their every need. This commitment is embodied in the company's motto, "We are Ladies and Gentlemen serving Ladies and Gentlemen," which emphasizes the importance of treating every guest with the utmost respect, courtesy, and care.

To deliver on this promise, the Ritz-Carlton empowers its employees (known as "Ladies and Gentlemen") to go above and beyond in serving guests. This empowerment is backed up by extensive training and support, as well as a company culture that prioritizes attention to detail and continuous improvement.

One of the key ways that the Ritz-Carlton pays attention to detail is through its "Gold Standards," a set of guiding principles and service standards that every employee is expected to know and embody. These standards cover everything from the proper way to answer the phone and greet guests to the specific steps for handling guest requests and complaints.

For example, one of the Ritz-Carlton's Gold Standards is "anticipate unexpressed needs." This means that employees are trained to look for subtle cues and opportunities to surprise and delight guests, even before they ask for something. This could be as simple as offering a cold towel and a refreshing drink to a guest who has just arrived from a long flight, or remembering a guest's favorite breakfast order and having it ready for them in the morning.

Another way that the Ritz-Carlton pays attention to detail is through its "daily line-up" meetings, where employees gather at the start of each shift to review the day's events, share guest feedback and preferences, and discuss ways to improve the guest experience. These meetings help to ensure that every employee is aligned around the same goals and standards, and that any issues or opportunities are quickly identified and addressed.

The Ritz-Carlton also relies heavily on guest feedback and data to drive continuous improvement. The company tracks a wide range of metrics, from guest satisfaction scores to employee engagement levels, and uses this data to identify areas for improvement and innovation. For example, if guest feedback indicates that a particular aspect of the room service experience is lacking, the company will quickly mobilize a team to analyze the issue and implement a solution.

This attention to detail extends to every aspect of the guest experience, from the design and maintenance of the physical property to the selection and training of employees. The Ritz-Carlton is known for its luxurious and well-appointed rooms, its impeccable cleanliness standards, and its courteous and attentive staff. Every detail, no matter how small, is carefully considered and executed with the goal of creating a seamless and memorable experience for guests.

The payoff for this attention to detail has been significant for the Ritz-Carlton. The company has consistently ranked among the top luxury hotel brands in the world, with a fiercely loyal customer base and a reputation for unparalleled service and quality. The Ritz-Carlton's success has also inspired other companies, both within the hospitality industry and beyond, to focus on the power of attention to detail in driving customer loyalty and business success.

The example of the Ritz-Carlton illustrates how the Principle of Attention to Detail can be applied not just to product design, but to every aspect of a company's operations and customer experience.

***

19

The Principle of Financial Management

In business strategy, the Principle of Financial Management is a critical component that underlies and supports all other aspects of a company's operations and decision-making. At its core, this principle emphasizes the importance of maintaining a strong financial foundation, making informed financial decisions, and aligning financial strategies with a company's overall goals and objectives.

Financial management encompasses a wide range of activities, from budgeting and forecasting to accounting and reporting, risk management, and investment analysis. Effective financial management enables companies to optimize their resources, minimize their risks, and create long-term value for their stakeholders.

One of the key aspects of the Principle of Financial Management is financial stability and discipline. Companies that prioritize financial stability are better positioned to weather economic downturns, invest in growth and innovation, and make strategic decisions with confidence. This requires a commitment to sound financial practices, such as maintaining adequate cash reserves, managing debt carefully, and avoiding excessive risk-taking.

Financial discipline also involves setting clear financial goals and metrics, and holding teams accountable for meeting those targets. This can include metrics such as revenue growth, profitability, cash flow, and return on investment. By tracking and analyzing these metrics regularly, companies can identify areas of strength and weakness, and make data-driven decisions about where to allocate resources and how to optimize performance.

Another critical aspect of the Principle of Financial Management is financial planning and forecasting. Effective financial planning involves creating a roadmap for a company's financial future, including projections for revenue, expenses, cash flow, and capital requirements. This requires a deep understanding of a company's business model, market trends, and competitive landscape, as well as the ability to anticipate and plan for potential risks and opportunities.

Financial forecasting is the process of using historical data and market analysis to predict future financial performance. By creating accurate and reliable financial forecasts, companies can make informed decisions about investments, resource allocation, and risk management. This can help companies to avoid overspending or underinvesting, and to optimize their financial performance over time.

Effective financial planning and forecasting also require a degree of flexibility and adaptability. In today's fast-paced and ever-changing business environment, companies need to be able to quickly adjust their financial strategies and tactics in response to new information, changing market conditions, or unexpected events. This requires a keen understanding of financial principles and tools, as well as the ability to think creatively and strategically about financial challenges and opportunities.

Another key aspect of the Principle of Financial Management is financial transparency and accountability. In today's business environment, stakeholders (including investors, customers, employees, and regulators) expect companies to be transparent and accountable about their financial performance and practices. This includes providing regular and accurate financial reports, disclosing material risks and uncertainties, and maintaining strong internal controls and governance practices.

Financial transparency and accountability are essential for building trust and credibility with stakeholders. When companies are open and honest about their financial performance and decision-making processes, they can foster a culture of trust and collaboration, which can lead to increased loyalty, investment, and support over time. Conversely, when companies are opaque or misleading about their financial practices, they risk damaging their reputation and losing the trust and confidence of their stakeholders.

Effective financial management also requires strong risk management practices. Every business faces a range of financial risks, from market volatility and economic downturns to credit defaults and fraud. Effective risk management involves identifying and assessing these risks, developing strategies to mitigate or manage them, and continuously monitoring and adjusting these strategies as needed.

One common risk management strategy is diversification, which involves spreading investments and resources across a range of different assets, markets, or business lines. By diversifying their portfolios, companies can reduce their exposure to any single risk factor and minimize the impact of potential losses. Another risk management strategy is hedging, which involves using financial instruments (such as derivatives or insurance policies) to offset potential losses from specific risks.

Effective risk management also requires a strong understanding of a company's risk tolerance and risk appetite. Some companies may be willing to take on higher levels of risk in pursuit of higher returns, while others may prioritize stability and predictability over growth. By aligning their risk management strategies with their overall business objectives and values, companies can make informed decisions about when and how to take on risk, and how to manage it effectively over time.

Another important aspect of the Principle of Financial Management is investment analysis and decision-making. Effective investment decision-making involves evaluating potential investments based on their expected returns, risks, and alignment with a company's overall strategy and goals. This requires a deep understanding of financial metrics and valuation techniques, as well as the ability to analyze market trends, competitive dynamics, and other relevant factors.

Investment analysis also involves considering the opportunity costs and trade-offs associated with different investment options. For example, investing in a new product line or market may require significant upfront costs and resources, which may limit a company's ability to invest in other areas or initiatives. By carefully weighing the potential benefits and risks of different investment options, and aligning them with a company's overall financial and strategic objectives, companies can make informed and value-creating investment decisions over time.

Lastly, the Principle of Financial Management emphasizes the importance of continuous learning and improvement. As business environments and financial markets continue to evolve and change, companies need to be able to adapt and grow their financial knowledge and capabilities over time. This requires ongoing investment in financial education and training, as well as a willingness to learn from past successes and failures.

One way that companies can foster continuous learning and improvement in financial management is by creating a culture of financial literacy and engagement across the organization. This can involve providing regular financial training and development opportunities for employees at all levels, as well as creating forums and channels for open communication and knowledge-sharing about financial topics and challenges.

Another way that companies can drive continuous improvement in financial management is by leveraging technology and data analytics to gain deeper insights and make more informed decisions. By using advanced financial modeling and forecasting tools, as well as real-time data and analytics platforms, companies can identify emerging trends, risks, and opportunities more quickly and accurately, and adjust their strategies and tactics accordingly.

In conclusion, by prioritizing financial stability and discipline, effective planning and forecasting, transparency and accountability, risk management, investment analysis, and continuous learning and improvement, companies can create a strong and sustainable financial foundation for long-term success.

* * *

20

The Principle of Cost Structure

In business strategy, the principle of cost structure plays a pivotal role in determining the success and sustainability of an organization. Cost structure refers to the various costs incurred by a company in the process of creating, delivering, and marketing its products or services. It encompasses fixed costs, variable costs, and overhead expenses, all of which contribute to the overall financial health and profitability of the business. When designing and planning a business strategy, it is imperative to carefully consider and optimize the cost structure to ensure long-term viability and competitiveness in the market.

One of the primary reasons why cost structure is so critical in business strategy is its direct impact on pricing and profitability. The costs incurred by a company ultimately determine the minimum price at which it can sell its products or services while still generating a profit. If the cost structure is not carefully managed, it can lead to higher prices that may not be competitive in the market, resulting in reduced sales and market share. On the other hand, a well-designed cost structure allows a company to offer competitive prices while still maintaining healthy profit margins.

To effectively optimize the cost structure, businesses must first gain a deep understanding of their various costs and how they contribute to the overall expenses. Fixed costs, such as rent, salaries, and equipment, remain relatively constant regardless of the level of production or sales. These costs must be carefully managed to ensure that they do not become a burden on the company's finances. Variable costs, such as raw materials and packaging, fluctuate based on the volume of production or sales. By identifying and controlling variable costs, businesses can improve their efficiency and reduce waste.

Overhead expenses, which include costs such as utilities, insurance, and administrative salaries, also play a significant role in the cost structure. While these expenses may not be directly tied to production or sales, they still impact the overall profitability of the company. By streamlining processes, implementing cost-saving measures, and negotiating better rates with suppliers and service providers, businesses can minimize overhead expenses and improve their bottom line.

Another crucial aspect of cost structure in business strategy is the concept of economies of scale. As a company grows and increases its production volume, it can often benefit from reduced costs per unit due to increased efficiency and the ability to negotiate better prices with suppliers. This is known as economies of scale, and it can provide a significant competitive advantage in the market. However, it is important to note that achieving economies of scale requires careful planning and investment in infrastructure, technology, and personnel.

In addition to internal cost management, businesses must also consider the cost structures of their competitors when developing their strategy. Understanding how rivals allocate their costs and price their products or services can provide valuable insights into the competitive landscape. By benchmarking against industry standards and identifying areas where the company can differentiate itself through cost advantages or unique value propositions, businesses can develop a more effective and sustainable strategy.

The principle of cost structure also plays a crucial role in decision-making processes related to outsourcing, automation, and vertical integration. Outsourcing certain functions or processes to third-party providers can help reduce costs and improve efficiency, but it also involves risks such as loss of control and potential quality issues. Automation, on the other hand, can streamline operations and reduce labor costs, but it requires significant upfront investment and may not be suitable for all types of businesses. Vertical integration, which involves acquiring or merging with suppliers or distributors, can provide greater control over the supply chain and potentially reduce costs, but it also comes with its own set of challenges and risks.

To effectively incorporate the principle of cost structure into business strategy, companies must adopt a data-driven approach. This involves regularly tracking and analyzing costs, identifying trends and anomalies, and making informed decisions based on the insights gained. By leveraging tools such as cost accounting, activity-based costing, and financial modeling, businesses can gain a clearer understanding of their cost structure and identify opportunities for optimization.

Furthermore, the principle of cost structure should be aligned with the overall goals and objectives of the business. For example, a company that aims to be the low-cost provider in its industry will need to place a greater emphasis on cost reduction and efficiency compared to a company that focuses on differentiation through premium products or services. By ensuring that the cost structure supports the overall strategic direction of the company, businesses can create a more cohesive and effective strategy.

Another important consideration in cost structure is the concept of cost-benefit analysis. This involves weighing the costs of a particular decision or investment against the potential benefits it can bring to the company. For example, investing in new technology or equipment may increase upfront costs but could lead to long-term cost savings and improved productivity. By carefully evaluating the costs and benefits of various initiatives, businesses can make more informed decisions that align with their strategic objectives.

In today's rapidly changing business environment, the principle of cost structure must also account for the impact of disruptive technologies and changing consumer preferences. The rise of e-commerce, mobile technology, and digital marketing has transformed the way businesses operate and interact with customers. To remain competitive, companies must adapt their cost structures to reflect these changes and invest in the necessary technologies and capabilities to meet evolving customer demands.

Moreover, the principle of cost structure should be viewed not just as a means to reduce expenses but also as an opportunity to create value for customers and stakeholders. By optimizing costs and improving efficiency, businesses can free up resources to invest in innovation, product development, and customer experience. This can lead to increased customer satisfaction, loyalty, and ultimately, long-term profitability.

To successfully implement the principle of cost structure in business strategy, it is essential to foster a culture of cost consciousness throughout the organization. This involves educating employees about the importance of cost management, encouraging them to identify cost-saving opportunities, and rewarding them for their contributions to cost optimization efforts. By engaging all levels of the organization in the cost management process, businesses can create a more sustainable and effective cost structure.

In conclusion, the principle of cost structure is a critical component of successful business strategy. By carefully considering and optimizing costs, businesses can improve their profitability, competitiveness, and long-term sustainability.

IKEA

IKEA has become a global success story, largely due to its effective implementation of the principle of cost structure in its business strategy.

IKEA's cost structure is built around the concept of offering affordable, well-designed furniture to the masses. To achieve this, the company has implemented several strategies that optimize costs at every stage of the value chain.

Firstly, IKEA has a unique product design approach that focuses on creating functional, modular furniture that can be easily packaged and transported. By designing products with efficient packaging in mind, IKEA can reduce shipping costs and minimize damage during transportation. This flat-pack design also allows customers to easily transport the furniture themselves, reducing IKEA's delivery costs.

Secondly, IKEA has a strong emphasis on supplier relationships and cost-effective sourcing. The company works closely with its suppliers to ensure that materials are sourced at the best possible prices without compromising quality. IKEA often purchases materials in bulk, leveraging its scale to negotiate favorable terms with suppliers. Additionally, the company has invested in its own manufacturing facilities in low-cost countries, allowing it to maintain tight control over production costs.

Thirdly, IKEA's store layout and self-service model are designed to minimize operational costs. The company's large, warehouse-style stores are located in suburban areas where real estate is less expensive. Customers are encouraged to browse the store, select their own items, and transport them home, reducing the need for sales associates and delivery personnel. This self-service model, combined with the flat-pack design, enables IKEA to maintain lower labor costs compared to traditional furniture retailers.

Furthermore, IKEA has embraced technology to streamline its operations and reduce costs. The company has invested heavily in its e-commerce platform, allowing customers to easily browse and purchase products online. This has helped IKEA expand its reach while minimizing the need for additional physical stores. The company has also implemented advanced inventory management systems and automation in its warehouses, reducing handling costs and improving efficiency.

IKEA's cost structure also benefits from its limited product range and standardization. By offering a carefully curated selection of products that are designed to be manufactured efficiently, IKEA can achieve economies of scale and reduce complexity in its operations. This standardization allows the company to maintain lower inventory levels and minimize waste, further reducing costs.

Despite its focus on cost optimization, IKEA has not compromised on quality or customer experience. The company invests in innovative product design and regularly updates its offerings to keep up with changing consumer preferences. IKEA also provides value-added services, such as home delivery and assembly, for customers who require them, creating additional revenue streams.

IKEA's success demonstrates how a well-designed cost structure can be a powerful competitive advantage. By optimizing costs at every stage of the value chain, from product design and sourcing to store operations and customer service, IKEA has been able to offer affordable, high-quality furniture to a global market. The company's cost structure strategy has not only helped it maintain profitability but has also allowed it to invest in growth and innovation, cementing its position as a leader in the furniture retail industry.

* * *

21

The Principle of Revenue Streams

Revenue streams refer to the various sources of income that a company generates through its business activities. These can include the sale of products or services, subscription fees, licensing, advertising, and more. A well-designed and diversified revenue stream strategy is essential for ensuring the long-term financial health and growth of a company.

At its core, the Principle of Revenue Streams is about creating value for customers while also capturing a fair share of that value for the company. This requires a deep understanding of customer needs, preferences, and willingness to pay, as well as a clear articulation of the company's unique value proposition and competitive differentiation. By aligning its revenue streams with its core strengths and strategic objectives, a company can create a virtuous cycle of growth and profitability that can withstand the test of time.

One of the primary reasons why the principle of revenue streams is so important in business strategy is that it directly impacts a company's ability to generate profits and sustain itself over time. A company with a single revenue stream is inherently more vulnerable to market fluctuations and disruptions compared to a company with multiple, diverse revenue streams. By having a variety of income sources, a business can mitigate risk and ensure a more stable and predictable cash flow.

When designing a revenue stream strategy, businesses must first identify their core offerings and value propositions. This involves understanding what products or services the company can provide that meet the needs and desires of its target market. Once these core offerings are identified, the company can explore various ways to monetize them and create revenue streams.

One common revenue stream strategy is the sale of products or services. This can include one-time purchases, such as a consumer buying a product from a retail store, or ongoing purchases, such as a subscription service. When implementing a product or service sales strategy, businesses must carefully consider factors such as pricing, distribution channels, and customer acquisition costs. Pricing should be based on a thorough understanding of the target market, competitive landscape, and production costs. Distribution channels should be chosen based on the most effective way to reach the target audience, whether through brick-and-mortar stores, e-commerce platforms, or direct sales. Customer acquisition costs, which include expenses such as marketing and advertising, must be carefully managed to ensure that the revenue generated from sales exceeds the cost of acquiring new customers.

Another popular revenue stream strategy is licensing or royalties. This involves granting permission to another party to use the company's intellectual property, such as patents, trademarks, or copyrights, in exchange for a fee or a percentage of revenue. Licensing can be an effective way for businesses to monetize their proprietary technology or brand without having to directly produce and sell products. However, it is important to carefully negotiate licensing agreements to ensure that the company's intellectual property is protected and that the terms of the agreement are favorable.

Advertising is another significant revenue stream for many businesses, particularly those in the media and entertainment industries. Companies can generate income by selling advertising space on their websites, in their publications, or during their broadcasts. The rise of digital advertising has created new opportunities for businesses to monetize their online presence through display ads, sponsored content, and affiliate marketing. To maximize advertising revenue, companies must have a deep understanding of their audience demographics, engagement metrics, and advertising industry trends.

Subscription-based models have also gained popularity in recent years, particularly in the software and entertainment industries. Under this model, customers pay a recurring fee, typically on a monthly or annual basis, to access a product or service. Subscription-based revenue streams can provide a more predictable and stable income compared to one-time sales, as customers are more likely to continue paying for a service they find valuable. However, businesses must continually innovate and improve their offerings to prevent customer churn and maintain a high retention rate.

In addition to these core revenue streams, businesses can also explore alternative income sources such as grants, sponsorships, and crowdfunding. Grants and sponsorships can provide a valuable source of funding for companies engaged in research, social impact projects, or events. Crowdfunding platforms have also emerged as a way for businesses to raise capital from a large number of individual investors, particularly for startups and creative projects.

To develop a successful revenue stream strategy, businesses must also consider the principle of diversification. Relying too heavily on a single revenue stream can leave a company vulnerable to market changes and competition. By diversifying their income sources, businesses can create a more resilient and adaptable financial model. However, diversification must be approached strategically, as spreading resources too thin across too many initiatives can lead to a lack of focus and effectiveness.

Another important aspect of the principle of revenue streams is the concept of pricing strategy. The prices a company sets for its products or services can have a significant impact on its ability to generate revenue and compete in the market. There are various pricing strategies businesses can employ, such as cost-plus pricing, value-based pricing, or dynamic pricing. Cost-plus pricing involves adding a markup to the cost of producing a product or service to determine the selling price. Value-based pricing, on the other hand, sets prices based on the perceived value of the offering to the customer, regardless of production costs. Dynamic pricing involves adjusting prices in real-time based on market demand and other factors. The choice of pricing strategy will depend on the company's industry, target market, and competitive landscape.

In today's data-driven business environment, the principle of revenue streams also requires a strong emphasis on analytics and metrics. Companies must regularly track and analyze their revenue performance, identifying trends, patterns, and opportunities for optimization. Key performance indicators (KPIs) such as customer lifetime value, customer acquisition cost, and revenue growth rate can provide valuable insights into the effectiveness of a company's revenue stream strategy. By leveraging data analytics tools and techniques, businesses can make informed decisions about pricing, marketing, and product development that can help maximize revenue and profitability.

Furthermore, the principle of revenue streams must be aligned with the overall goals and objectives of the business. A company's revenue strategy should support its mission, values, and long-term vision. For example, a company that prioritizes environmental sustainability may choose to focus on revenue streams that promote eco-friendly products or services, even if they may not be as immediately profitable as other options. By ensuring that revenue streams are consistent with the company's core identity and purpose, businesses can create a more authentic and compelling brand that resonates with customers and stakeholders.

In conclusion, the principle of revenue streams is a critical component of successful business strategy. By carefully designing and diversifying their income sources, businesses can create a more stable, predictable, and profitable financial model.

Apple

Apple is renowned for its innovative products, including the iPhone, iPad, Mac computers, and various services like Apple Music, Apple TV+, and iCloud. The company's revenue stream strategy is built around a diverse mix of hardware sales, software and services, and licensing.

One of Apple's primary revenue streams is the sale of its hardware products. The iPhone, in particular, has been a major driver of Apple's revenue growth

THE PRINCIPLE OF REVENUE STREAMS

since its introduction in 2007. By continuously innovating and releasing new models with improved features and functionality, Apple has been able to maintain a loyal customer base and attract new users. The company's pricing strategy for iPhones has been a key factor in its success, with a range of models at different price points to cater to various market segments. Apple's other hardware products, such as the iPad, Mac, and Apple Watch, also contribute significantly to its revenue.

In addition to hardware sales, Apple has successfully diversified its revenue streams through its growing services business. This includes digital content stores like the App Store, Apple Music, and Apple TV+, as well as cloud storage services like iCloud. By offering a wide range of services that integrate seamlessly with its hardware products, Apple has created a powerful ecosystem that keeps users engaged and encourages them to stay within the Apple brand. The company's services revenue has been growing rapidly in recent years, providing a more stable and predictable income stream compared to the cyclical nature of hardware sales.

Another important revenue stream for Apple is licensing. The company licenses its proprietary technology and intellectual property to other companies, such as the use of its Apple Pay payment system by third-party apps and websites. Apple also earns revenue from licensing its brand and logo for use on third-party accessories, such as iPhone cases and headphones. By leveraging its strong brand reputation and technological expertise, Apple can generate significant income from licensing without having to directly produce and sell these products.

Apple's revenue stream strategy also benefits from its strong brand loyalty and customer retention. The company's products and services are designed to work seamlessly together, creating a cohesive user experience that encourages customers to stay within the Apple ecosystem. This loyalty is reinforced through initiatives like the Apple Upgrade Program, which allows customers to easily upgrade to new iPhone models each year, and the Apple Card, a credit card that offers rewards and benefits for Apple purchases.

Furthermore, Apple has been able to successfully enter new markets and create new revenue streams through strategic partnerships and acquisitions.

For example, the company's partnership with Goldman Sachs to launch the Apple Card has allowed it to enter the financial services market and generate revenue through interest and transaction fees. Apple's acquisition of Beats Electronics in 2014 also helped it expand its presence in the music streaming and headphone markets.

As Apple continues to innovate and expand its product and service offerings, its revenue stream strategy will likely evolve to capitalize on new opportunities in emerging markets such as augmented reality, artificial intelligence, and the Internet of Things. By maintaining a diverse and adaptable revenue stream mix, Apple can continue to deliver value to its customers and shareholders, cementing its position as a leader in the technology industry.

* * *

22

The Principle of Culture

In the world of business, where competition is fierce and the stakes are high, crafting a successful strategy is an art that requires a delicate balance of various principles. Among these principles, the Principle of Culture stands tall, serving as a fundamental pillar that shapes the very essence of an organization. Culture, the invisible yet potent force that permeates every aspect of a company, is the secret ingredient that can make or break a business strategy.

At its core, culture encompasses the shared values, beliefs, attitudes, and behaviors that define an organization. It is the unwritten code that guides employees in their daily interactions, decision-making processes, and overall approach to work. A strong, well-defined culture acts as a compass, ensuring that every member of the organization is aligned and working towards a common goal.

When it comes to building a successful business strategy, culture plays a multifaceted role. It influences the formulation of the strategy itself, serving as a lens through which leaders evaluate strategic options. A culture that values innovation, for example, will naturally gravitate towards strategies that prioritize research and development, while a culture that emphasizes customer-centricity will place the needs and preferences of customers at the forefront of strategic decision-making.

But culture's impact extends far beyond the realm of strategy formulation.

It is also a critical factor in the successful execution of a strategy. A culture that fosters open communication, collaboration, and trust creates an environment where employees feel empowered to take ownership of their roles and contribute their best efforts towards achieving the company's strategic objectives. When employees are engaged and motivated, they are more likely to go above and beyond, driving the organization forward with their dedication and passion.

Moreover, a strong culture can be a powerful differentiator in the marketplace. In a world where products and services can be easily replicated, culture becomes the unique fingerprint that sets a company apart from its competitors. It is the intangible asset that attracts top talent, retains loyal customers, and builds a positive reputation in the industry. A company known for its innovative culture, for instance, will naturally attract creative minds who thrive in an environment that encourages out-of-the-box thinking. Similarly, a company with a culture of exceptional customer service will earn the trust and loyalty of its customers, creating a sustainable competitive advantage.

However, building and maintaining a culture that supports a successful business strategy is no easy feat. It requires intentional effort, consistent reinforcement, and unwavering commitment from leadership. Leaders must not only articulate the desired culture but also embody it in their own actions and decisions. They must create an environment that encourages the behaviors and mindsets that align with the company's strategic goals, while also being willing to address and correct any deviations from the desired culture.

One of the key challenges in leveraging culture for strategic success is ensuring that it remains relevant and adaptable in the face of change. As businesses navigate the ever-shifting landscape of their industries, their strategies must evolve to stay ahead of the curve. Culture, too, must be agile enough to support these strategic pivots. This requires a delicate balance between preserving the core values that define the organization and embracing the flexibility needed to adapt to new realities.

To achieve this balance, companies must foster a culture of continuous learning and growth. Encouraging employees to embrace change, experiment with new ideas, and learn from both successes and failures creates a resilient and adaptable culture that can weather the storms of change. It is through this ongoing process of learning and evolution that a culture can remain a source of strategic strength, rather than a hindrance to progress.

Ultimately, the Principle of Culture reminds us that a successful business strategy is not just about the numbers, the market analysis, or the competitive landscape. It is also about the people who bring that strategy to life. It is about creating an environment where individuals can thrive, where their unique talents and perspectives are valued, and where they are inspired to give their best to the organization. When a company gets its culture right, it unleashes a powerful force that propels it towards success, one that competitors may find difficult to replicate.

Southwest Airlines

Founded in 1967, Southwest Airlines has consistently been one of the most profitable and successful airlines in the United States, despite operating in a highly competitive and challenging industry. At the heart of Southwest's success lies its strong and distinctive organizational culture.

From its inception, Southwest Airlines has cultivated a culture that prioritizes employee happiness, customer satisfaction, and operational efficiency. The company's core values, which include a warrior spirit, a servant's heart, and a fun-loving attitude, are not just mere slogans but are deeply ingrained in every aspect of the organization.

Southwest's culture of putting employees first has been a key driver of its success. The company believes that happy employees lead to happy customers, which in turn leads to business success. This philosophy is evident in the way Southwest treats its employees. The company provides comprehensive benefits, competitive salaries, and opportunities for growth and development. It also fosters a sense of camaraderie and teamwork among its employees, encouraging them to have fun on the job and celebrate each other's successes.

This employee-centric culture has translated into exceptional customer service, which has become a hallmark of Southwest's brand. The company's employees are known for their friendly, helpful, and often humorous interactions with customers. They go above and beyond to ensure that passengers have a positive experience, whether it's helping with luggage, entertaining children, or even singing the safety instructions. This level of customer service has earned Southwest a loyal following and has differentiated the airline from its competitors.

Moreover, Southwest's culture of operational efficiency has been critical to its ability to execute its low-cost business strategy. The company is known for its lean operations, quick turnaround times, and no-frills service. Employees are trained to work efficiently and effectively, with a focus on minimizing waste and maximizing productivity. This culture of efficiency has allowed Southwest to keep its costs low while still providing reliable and high-quality service to its customers.

Southwest's culture has also been instrumental in its ability to adapt and innovate in the face of challenges. When the airline industry faced a crisis following the September 11th attacks in 2001, Southwest was one of the few airlines that remained profitable. The company's culture of resilience, flexibility, and creativity allowed it to quickly adjust its operations and find new ways to serve its customers. For example, Southwest introduced a "Friends Fly Free" promotion, which encouraged people to travel and helped to fill empty seats during a difficult time.

Over the years, Southwest has continued to leverage its strong culture to support its business strategy. The company has expanded its route network, introduced new services such as Business Select, and even acquired AirTran Airways, all while staying true to its core values and cultural principles. Today, Southwest is the largest domestic carrier in the United States, serving over 100 destinations and carrying more than 130 million passengers annually.

The success of Southwest Airlines is a testament to the power of a strong and aligned organizational culture. By fostering a culture that prioritizes employee happiness, customer satisfaction, and operational efficiency, Southwest has been able to execute its low-cost business strategy with remarkable effectiveness. The company's culture has been a source of sustainable competitive advantage, allowing it to differentiate itself in a crowded market and build a loyal customer base.

Southwest's example also highlights the importance of leadership in shaping and maintaining a strong culture. The company's founders, Herb Kelleher and Rollin King, were instrumental in defining Southwest's culture and values from the very beginning. They led by example, embodying the behaviors and attitudes they wanted to see in their employees. Subsequent leaders, such as Gary Kelly and Bob Jordan, have continued to reinforce and build upon this cultural foundation, ensuring that it remains relevant and vital to the organization's success.

In conclusion, the case of Southwest Airlines illustrates how a strong and well-aligned organizational culture can be a powerful enabler of business strategy. By creating a culture that supports and enhances its strategic objectives, Southwest has been able to achieve remarkable success in a challenging industry.

* * *

23

The Principle of Branding

Branding is not merely a superficial aspect of a company; it is a fundamental element that permeates every facet of the organization, shaping its identity, reputation, and long-term success. By incorporating branding into the core of the business strategy, companies can differentiate themselves, create enduring customer loyalty, and navigate the challenges of an ever-evolving market landscape.

At its essence, branding is the art of creating a unique and compelling identity for a company, product, or service. It encompasses the visual elements, such as logos and packaging, as well as the intangible qualities, such as values, personality, and customer experience. A strong brand is more than just a recognizable name or symbol; it is a promise to customers, a reflection of the company's purpose, and a differentiator in a crowded marketplace.

By integrating branding into the foundation of the business strategy, companies can ensure that all subsequent decisions, actions, and initiatives align with the brand's core identity and purpose. This cohesive approach helps to build a consistent and memorable brand experience across all touchpoints, reinforcing the company's positioning and value proposition in the minds of customers.

Failure to prioritize branding in the strategy development process can lead to dire consequences. Without a strong brand identity, companies risk becoming commoditized, interchangeable with competitors, and vulnerable to market fluctuations. In a commoditized market, price becomes the primary differentiator, leading to a race to the bottom and eroding profit margins. Moreover, a lack of branding leaves a company exposed to external factors, such as economic downturns, industry disruptions, or shifts in consumer preferences.

To illustrate the power of branding, let's consider a seemingly simple product: eggs. In a traditional market, eggs are often perceived as a commodity, with little differentiation between producers. However, by incorporating branding into the business strategy, an egg company can transform its product into a distinct and desirable offering. By developing a unique brand identity, emphasizing factors such as quality, freshness, sustainability, or ethical farming practices, the company can create a compelling narrative that resonates with consumers.

Branded eggs can command a premium price, as customers associate the brand with superior attributes and are willing to pay more for the perceived value. Moreover, a strong egg brand can weather challenges such as a bird flu outbreak or changing consumer preferences. By building a loyal customer base and establishing trust in the brand, the company can maintain its market position and even thrive in the face of adversity.

One company that has successfully embraced the Principle of Branding is Intel. Despite the fact that its products are often hidden from view, installed inside computers and other devices, Intel has managed to build one of the most recognizable and valuable brands in the world. Through consistent and strategic branding efforts, Intel has positioned itself as the leading provider of high-performance, reliable, and innovative microprocessors, solidifying its position as a titan in the tech industry.

Intel's success in branding can be attributed to several key factors. Firstly, the company has invested significantly in creating a strong visual identity, with its iconic "Intel Inside" logo and distinctive five-note jingle becoming instantly recognizable to consumers worldwide. Intel has also been a trailblazer in co-branding, partnering with major computer manufacturers like Dell, HP, and Lenovo to prominently feature its logo on their products and packaging.

Beyond its visual identity, Intel has also been strategic in its messaging and positioning. The company has consistently emphasized the performance, reliability, and innovation of its products, highlighting their ability to power the most advanced and cutting-edge technology. Intel has also been a leader in corporate social responsibility, investing in initiatives related to education, environmental sustainability, and diversity and inclusion, further enhancing its reputation and appeal to socially conscious consumers.

Another key aspect of Intel's branding success has been its ability to evolve and adapt over time. As the technology landscape has shifted and new competitors have emerged, Intel has been proactive in updating its brand identity and messaging to remain relevant and compelling to customers. For example, in recent years, the company has placed a greater emphasis on its role in enabling artificial intelligence, 5G networks, and other emerging technologies, positioning itself as a pioneer in the new era of computing.

To successfully integrate branding into the business strategy, companies must allocate resources and plan accordingly. This includes investing in market research to understand target audiences, developing a clear brand positioning and messaging, and creating a consistent visual identity across all marketing materials. It also involves aligning internal processes, such as product development, customer service, and employee training, to ensure that the brand promise is delivered consistently at every interaction.

Furthermore, the Principle of Branding requires ongoing investment and management. Building a strong brand is not a one-time exercise; it requires continuous nurturing, monitoring, and adaptation. Companies must regularly assess their brand's performance, gather customer feedback, and stay attuned to market trends and competitor activities. By consistently delivering on the brand promise and evolving with the changing needs and preferences of customers, companies can maintain the relevance and vitality of their brand over time.

In today's digital age, branding has become even more crucial. With the proliferation of online channels and social media, companies have unprecedented opportunities to engage with customers, build brand communities, and foster emotional connections. However, this also means that branding efforts must extend beyond traditional marketing and encompass digital strategies, such as content marketing, influencer partnerships, and social media engagement. By creating a seamless and compelling brand experience across both online and offline touchpoints, companies can amplify their brand's reach and impact.

Ultimately, the Principle of Branding is about creating a lasting impression in the minds of customers, differentiating the company from competitors, and building enduring relationships based on trust, loyalty, and shared values. By weaving branding into the fabric of the business strategy, companies can create a powerful and resilient foundation for long-term success.

* * *

24

The Principle of Rapid Prototyping, Testing, and Iteration

In the world of business, the ability to quickly develop, test, and refine ideas is essential for staying ahead of the competition and achieving long-term success. The Principle of Rapid Prototyping, Testing, and Iteration emphasizes the importance of creating tangible prototypes, gathering feedback, and continuously improving upon a product or strategy to ensure its viability and effectiveness in the market.

At its core, this principle is about embracing a culture of experimentation and learning. Rather than spending months or years perfecting a product or strategy in isolation, companies that adhere to this principle understand the value of putting their ideas out into the world as soon as possible, even if they are not yet fully polished. By creating a prototype – whether it's a physical product, a software application, or a new business process – companies can gather invaluable feedback from customers, partners, and other stakeholders, and use that feedback to iterate and improve upon their initial concept.

One company that has embraced the Principle of Rapid Prototyping, Testing, and Iteration to great effect is Dropbox. When the company was first founded, its initial product was a simple tool for syncing files across multiple computers. However, rather than spending years trying to perfect this tool in-house, Dropbox quickly released a prototype to a small group of users and began gathering feedback. Based on this feedback, the company rapidly iterated on its product, adding new features and functionality in response to user needs and preferences.

Over time, this approach has allowed Dropbox to stay ahead of the curve and maintain its position as a leader in the cloud storage and collaboration space. By constantly experimenting with new ideas and gathering feedback from its users, the company has been able to innovate and evolve at a rapid pace, introducing new products and services that anticipate and meet the changing needs of its customers.

Another key benefit of the Principle of Rapid Prototyping, Testing, and Iteration is that it allows companies to fail fast and learn from their mistakes. In traditional product development cycles, companies often invest significant time and resources into perfecting a product before releasing it to the market, only to discover that it fails to resonate with customers or meet their needs. By contrast, companies that embrace rapid prototyping and testing can quickly identify what works and what doesn't, and pivot their strategies accordingly.

This approach also allows companies to be more agile and responsive to changing market conditions and customer needs. By constantly gathering feedback and iterating on their products and strategies, companies can stay ahead of the curve and adapt to new challenges and opportunities as they arise. This is particularly important in today's fast-paced business environment, where the pace of change is accelerating and companies that fail to adapt risk being left behind.

Of course, implementing the Principle of Rapid Prototyping, Testing, and Iteration is not always easy. It requires a significant shift in mindset and culture, as well as a willingness to embrace failure and learn from it. Companies must also invest in the tools and processes necessary to support rapid experimentation and iteration, such as agile development methodologies, user testing platforms, and data analytics capabilities.

In conclusion, the Principle of Rapid Prototyping, Testing, and Iteration is a critical component of any successful business strategy in today's fast-paced and ever-changing business environment. By embracing a culture of experimentation and learning, companies can quickly develop and refine their products and strategies, gather valuable feedback from customers and stakeholders, and stay ahead of the competition.

Netflix

When Netflix first launched in 1997, its primary business model was a DVD-by-mail rental service. However, as the company grew and technology evolved, Netflix recognized the potential for streaming video content over the internet. Rather than making a sudden and complete shift in strategy, Netflix began experimenting with streaming video as a complementary offering to its DVD rental service.

Initially, Netflix's streaming service was limited in scope and availability, with only a small selection of titles and compatibility with a handful of devices. However, the company used this initial prototype to gather valuable feedback from its customers and learn about their viewing habits and preferences. Based on this feedback, Netflix rapidly iterated on its streaming service, expanding its content library, improving its user interface, and adding support for a wider range of devices.

Over time, Netflix's streaming service became the company's primary focus, eclipsing its DVD rental business in terms of both revenue and subscriber growth. By continually experimenting with new features and gathering data on user behavior, Netflix was able to refine its recommendation algorithms, personalize its content offerings, and create a seamless and engaging viewing experience for its customers.

Netflix's embrace of rapid prototyping and iteration has also extended to its original content strategy. When the company first began producing its own television shows and movies, it took a data-driven approach, using viewer data to inform its creative decisions and optimize its content investments. This approach has allowed Netflix to create a diverse and popular library of original programming, with hits like "Stranger Things," "Narcos," and "The Crown" that have attracted millions of subscribers worldwide.

Perhaps most importantly, Netflix's culture of experimentation and iteration has allowed the company to remain agile and adapt to changing market conditions and consumer preferences. As new competitors have entered the streaming video space and consumer viewing habits have evolved, Netflix has continued to innovate and experiment with new formats, pricing models, and content strategies. By remaining open to change and embracing the Principle of Rapid Prototyping, Testing, and Iteration, Netflix has been able to maintain its position as a leader in the digital entertainment industry.

* * *

25

The Principle of Execution

In business strategy, the principle of execution is a critical factor that separates successful companies from those that struggle to achieve their goals. Execution refers to the ability of an organization to effectively implement its strategies, plans, and initiatives in a timely and efficient manner. It is the bridge between a company's vision and its actual results, and it requires a combination of strong leadership, clear communication, resource allocation, and performance management.

One of the primary reasons why the principle of execution is so important in business strategy is that even the most well-conceived plans are worthless if they cannot be successfully implemented. Many companies invest significant time and resources into developing comprehensive strategies, but fail to execute them effectively due to a variety of factors such as lack of alignment, inadequate resources, or poor communication. As a result, these companies may miss out on valuable opportunities, lose market share to competitors, or fail to achieve their desired outcomes.

To successfully execute a business strategy, companies must first ensure that their plans are clearly defined and communicated throughout the organization. This involves setting specific, measurable, achievable, relevant, and time-bound (SMART) goals that align with the company's overall vision and objectives. These goals should be cascaded down to every level of the organization, so that each employee understands their role and responsibilities in contributing to the company's success.

Effective communication is also critical to the principle of execution. Leaders must be able to articulate the company's strategy and goals in a way that is easily understood by all stakeholders, including employees, customers, partners, and investors. This requires regular and transparent communication through various channels such as meetings, emails, newsletters, and town halls. By keeping everyone informed and engaged, companies can foster a sense of ownership and accountability that drives execution forward.

Execution becomes easier when employees and other stakeholders are involved in idea generation, suggestions, and decision-making processes. Even if their specific ideas are not ultimately chosen, the fact that they had the opportunity to contribute and that their ideas were listened to can significantly improve buy-in and motivation. When people feel that their opinions are valued, they are more likely to work hard in executing the chosen strategy.

Another important aspect of execution is educating employees to see the big picture and understand how their individual work impacts various parts of the organization. By helping employees learn about the business as a whole and how their roles fit into the larger context, companies can foster a deeper sense of engagement and ownership. When employees clearly see the connection between their efforts and the company's success, they are more likely to be invested in the outcome and committed to executing the strategy effectively.

Resource allocation is another key aspect of the principle of execution. Companies must ensure that they have the necessary resources, including people, technology, and capital, to effectively implement their strategies. This requires careful planning and budgeting to allocate resources in a way that aligns with the company's priorities and goals. It also involves making tough decisions about which initiatives to prioritize and which to defer or eliminate based on their potential impact and feasibility.

Performance management is also essential to the principle of execution. Companies must regularly monitor and measure their progress against their goals and objectives, using key performance indicators (KPIs) and other metrics. This allows them to identify areas of strength and weakness, and make adjustments as needed to stay on track. Performance management also involves providing feedback and recognition to employees who are contributing to the company's success, as well as addressing any performance issues that may be hindering execution.

One of the key challenges in executing a business strategy is managing change and uncertainty. As market conditions, customer preferences, and competitive landscapes evolve, companies must be able to adapt and pivot their strategies accordingly. This requires a culture of agility and innovation, where employees are encouraged to experiment, take risks, and learn from failures. It also requires strong leadership that can navigate complex challenges and make tough decisions in the face of uncertainty.

To illustrate the principle of execution in action, let's consider the example of a company that has developed a new product that it believes will revolutionize its industry. The company has invested significant resources into research and development, and has a clear vision for how the product will be marketed and sold. However, when it comes time to launch the product, the company faces numerous challenges, including production delays, supply chain disruptions, and unexpected competition from rivals.

In this scenario, the company's ability to execute its strategy will be critical to its success. The leadership team must quickly assess the situation and make decisions about how to allocate resources and adapt their plans accordingly. They may need to work closely with suppliers and partners to resolve production issues, or adjust their marketing and sales strategies to better differentiate their product from competitors. They may also need to communicate transparently with employees and customers about any delays or changes to the launch timeline.

Throughout this process, the company must remain focused on its ultimate goal of successfully launching and scaling the new product. This requires a combination of discipline, flexibility, and resilience in the face of challenges and setbacks. By staying aligned around a clear vision and strategy, and empowering employees to take ownership and initiative, the company can navigate the uncertainties of execution and ultimately achieve its desired outcomes.

Another key aspect of the principle of execution is the importance of continuous improvement and learning. Even the most successful companies must continually evaluate and optimize their strategies and operations to stay ahead of the curve. This requires a culture of curiosity, experimentation, and data-driven decision making, where employees are encouraged to ask questions, challenge assumptions, and propose new ideas.

One way that companies can foster continuous improvement is through regular retrospectives and post-mortems, where teams reflect on their successes and failures and identify opportunities for improvement. This can involve analyzing data and metrics to identify trends and patterns, as well as gathering qualitative feedback from employees, customers, and other stakeholders. By institutionalizing a process of continuous learning and iteration, companies can stay agile and adaptable in the face of changing market conditions and customer needs.

Finally, the principle of execution requires a deep understanding of the company's core competencies and competitive advantages. Companies must be able to identify and leverage their unique strengths and capabilities in order to execute their strategies effectively. This may involve focusing on a specific market niche, developing proprietary technologies or processes, or building strong relationships with customers and partners.

At the same time, companies must also be aware of their limitations and weaknesses, and take steps to address them through strategic investments, partnerships, or acquisitions. By honestly assessing their capabilities and gaps, and making deliberate choices about where to focus their resources and efforts, companies can position themselves for long-term success and sustainability.

In conclusion, the principle of execution requires a combination of clear vision, effective communication, resource allocation, performance management, employee engagement, and continuous improvement. Companies that can master the art of execution are able to turn their plans and ideas into tangible results, and outperform their competitors in the marketplace.

* * *

26

The Principle of Storytelling

In the world of business strategy, the principle of storytelling is often overlooked, yet it holds immense power in captivating audiences, inspiring action, and driving success. At its core, storytelling is the art of crafting a compelling narrative that resonates with people on an emotional level. It goes beyond mere facts and figures, tapping into the human experience and creating a shared sense of purpose and meaning.

Imagine a company that has developed a groundbreaking new product, one that has the potential to revolutionize its industry and change people's lives for the better. The company's leaders have poured their hearts and souls into this project, investing countless hours and resources to bring it to fruition. They have a clear vision of what they want to achieve and a deep understanding of the problem they are trying to solve.

However, having a great product is only half the battle. To truly succeed, the company must be able to communicate its vision and value proposition in a way that captures the imagination and inspires others to join the cause. This is where the principle of storytelling comes into play.

The company's leaders must craft a narrative that brings their product to life, one that showcases its unique features and benefits, and articulates how it will make a difference in people's lives. They must paint a vivid picture of the problem they are solving and the impact their solution will have on the world. They must create a sense of urgency and excitement, making people feel like they are part of something bigger than themselves.

To do this, the company must first understand its audience. Who are the people they are trying to reach? What are their needs, desires, and pain points? What motivates and inspires them? By answering these questions, the company can tailor its story to resonate with its target audience on a deep, emotional level.

The company must also be authentic and transparent in its storytelling. People can quickly spot inauthenticity, and nothing erodes trust faster than a story that feels contrived or manipulative. The company's story must be grounded in truth and reflect its core values and beliefs. It must be a genuine expression of who the company is and what it stands for.

Once the company has crafted its story, it must then find ways to share it with the world. This can take many forms, from social media and content marketing to public speaking and thought leadership. The key is to be consistent and persistent in telling the story, to keep it fresh and relevant, and to adapt it as needed to meet the changing needs of the audience.

One company that has mastered the art of storytelling is Apple. From its early days, Apple has been a master at crafting compelling narratives that capture the imagination and inspire devotion among its customers. Apple's stories are not just about its products, but about the values and ideals that those products represent. Apple's stories are about creativity, innovation, and the power of technology to change the world.

Think back to the launch of the original iPhone in 2007. Steve Jobs took the stage and began by talking about how Apple had always been at the intersection of technology and the liberal arts, of creativity and innovation. He spoke about how the iPhone was a revolutionary device that would change the way people communicate and access information. He painted a picture of a world where people could carry the internet in their pockets, where they could connect with loved ones across the globe, and where they could access a world of knowledge and entertainment at their fingertips.

Jobs' story was not just about the features and specs of the iPhone, but about the possibilities it unlocked and the impact it would have on people's lives. It was a story that resonated with people on an emotional level, that made them feel like they were part of something special and important. And it worked. The iPhone went on to become one of the most successful products in history, transforming not just the mobile phone industry, but the way we live and work.

Apple's storytelling prowess extends beyond product launches. The company has consistently used storytelling to build its brand and cultivate a loyal following. From its iconic "Think Different" campaign to its "Shot on iPhone" series, Apple has always found ways to tell stories that showcase the creativity and ingenuity of its customers and the ways in which its products enable and inspire them.

Of course, storytelling is not just about building brand loyalty and selling products. It is also a powerful tool for driving organizational change and aligning teams around a shared vision and purpose. When leaders can articulate a compelling story about where the organization is headed and why it matters, they can inspire their teams to work together towards a common goal, even in the face of challenges and setbacks.

One leader who exemplified this was Dr. Martin Luther King Jr. King's "I Have a Dream" speech is one of the most powerful examples of storytelling in history. In just a few short minutes, King painted a vivid picture of a world where people of all races and backgrounds could live together in harmony, where children could hold hands and sing together without regard for the color of their skin. He spoke about the challenges and injustices faced by African Americans, but also about the hope and possibility of a better future.

King's story was not just a speech, but a call to action. It inspired millions of people to join the civil rights movement and work towards a more just and equitable society. It gave people a sense of purpose and meaning, a reason to keep fighting even in the face of adversity. And it changed the course of history.

The principle of storytelling is not just about crafting a compelling narrative, but about using that narrative to drive action and create change. It is about tapping into the power of emotion and imagination to inspire people to think differently, to see new possibilities, and to work together towards a shared vision of the future.

As business leaders, we have a responsibility to use storytelling to create positive change in the world. We have the power to shape the narrative around our products, our companies, and our industries. We can use our stories to build bridges, to create understanding, and to drive progress on the issues that matter most.

But to do this, we must be willing to be vulnerable, to share our own stories and experiences, and to listen to the stories of others. We must be willing to have difficult conversations and to confront hard truths. We must be willing to lead with empathy and compassion, to see the humanity in others and to work towards a world where everyone can thrive.

Ultimately, the principle of storytelling is about connection. It is about building relationships and creating a shared sense of purpose and meaning. It is about tapping into the power of narrative to inspire action and drive change. And it is about using our stories to create a better world, one where everyone can find their place and make their mark.

So let us embrace the power of storytelling in our business strategies and in our lives. Let us craft compelling narratives that inspire and engage, that create understanding and drive progress. Let us use our stories to build a brighter future, one where everyone can thrive and where anything is possible. For in the end, it is our stories that will shape the world we leave behind.

Airbnb

Founded in 2008 by Brian Chesky, Joe Gebbia, and Nathan Blecharczyk, Airbnb started as a simple idea: to provide affordable accommodations for travelers by connecting them with locals who had extra space in their homes. But from the very beginning, Airbnb was more than just a platform for booking rooms. It was a story about belonging, about the power of human connection, and about the transformative nature of travel.

Airbnb's story began with the founders' own experiences as travelers. They understood the challenges of finding affordable accommodations in expensive cities, and they saw an opportunity to create a new kind of travel experience, one that was more authentic, more personal, and more meaningful than staying in a traditional hotel.

To bring this vision to life, Airbnb crafted a compelling narrative around the idea of belonging. The company's mission was not just to provide a place to stay, but to create a sense of connection and community among travelers and hosts alike. Airbnb's marketing campaigns featured stories of real people and real experiences, showcasing the unique personalities and passions of hosts from around the world.

One of the most powerful examples of Airbnb's storytelling prowess was its "Live There" campaign, launched in 2016. The campaign featured a series of short films that followed travelers as they immersed themselves in local communities and experienced life like a local. The films were shot in a documentary style, capturing authentic moments of connection and discovery, and showcasing the transformative power of travel.

The "Live There" campaign was more than just a marketing initiative. It was a statement of Airbnb's values and a reflection of its core mission. By telling stories of real people and real experiences, Airbnb was able to create a sense of belonging and community that extended beyond the platform itself. It inspired travelers to seek out more authentic and meaningful experiences, and it encouraged hosts to open their homes and their hearts to strangers from around the world.

Airbnb's storytelling efforts have not been limited to its marketing campaigns. The company has also used storytelling to navigate challenges and controversies, such as concerns around safety and discrimination on the platform. In response to these issues, Airbnb has launched initiatives like its "Open Homes" program, which provides free housing to refugees and disaster survivors, and its "Community Commitment," which requires all users to pledge to treat everyone with respect and without judgment or bias.

By telling stories of compassion and inclusion, Airbnb has been able to build trust and credibility with its users and stakeholders, even in the face of difficult challenges. It has demonstrated a commitment to its values and a willingness to take action to create positive change in the world.

As business leaders, we can learn from Airbnb's example and embrace the power of storytelling in our own organizations. We can use stories to build brands, to inspire teams, and to drive positive change in the world. We can tell stories that showcase our values and our mission, that celebrate the unique experiences and perspectives of our customers and employees, and that create a sense of belonging and purpose that extends beyond the walls of our companies.

Apple's 1984 Advertisement: The Story of Rebellion

In 1984, Apple unveiled a groundbreaking advertisement that would forever change the landscape of technology marketing. The commercial, directed by Ridley Scott, was a cinematic masterpiece that told a powerful story of rebellion against conformity and the status quo.

The advertisement opens with a dystopian scene reminiscent of George Orwell's novel, "1984." A sea of people, dressed in drab, uniform clothing, marches in unison towards a giant screen where a Big Brother-like figure delivers a speech about the virtues of conformity and the evils of individuality. The audience sits motionless, their faces devoid of emotion, as they absorb the oppressive message.

Suddenly, a lone figure emerges from the crowd. It is a young woman, dressed in vibrant athletic wear, running towards the screen with a sledgehammer in hand. As she races through the hall, she is pursued by armed guards, symbolizing the forces of oppression and control.

With a triumphant leap, the woman hurls the sledgehammer towards the screen, shattering it in a burst of light and smoke. As the screen explodes, the audience is awakened from their trance, their faces filled with shock and awe.

The advertisement closes with a simple yet powerful message: "On January 24th, Apple Computer will introduce Macintosh. And you'll see why 1984 won't be like '1984.'"

The story told in Apple's 1984 advertisement is one of rebellion against conformity and the status quo. It positions Apple as the underdog, the brave challenger taking on the monolithic IBM and its stranglehold on the personal computer market. By aligning itself with the values of individuality, creativity, and freedom, Apple tapped into the aspirations of a generation that yearned to break free from the constraints of corporate America.

The advertisement's impact was immediate and far-reaching. It created a buzz around the launch of the Macintosh and established Apple as a brand that stood for something greater than just technology. It was a declaration of war against the bland, boxy computers of the time and a rallying cry for a new era of personal computing.

Warby Parker: The Story of Socially Conscious Eyewear

Warby Parker is a company that has built its brand around a compelling story of social responsibility and customer empowerment. Founded in 2010 by four friends at the Wharton School of Business, Warby Parker was born out of a frustration with the high cost and limited options of traditional eyewear retailers.

The company's story begins with a simple premise: that everyone deserves access to high-quality, stylish eyewear at an affordable price. By cutting out the middlemen and designing its own frames, Warby Parker is able to offer its customers prescription glasses for a fraction of the cost of traditional retailers.

But Warby Parker's story goes beyond just disrupting the eyewear industry. The company has a deep commitment to social responsibility and has made giving back a core part of its business model. For every pair of glasses sold, Warby Parker donates a pair to someone in need through its "Buy a Pair, Give a Pair" program.

This program has become a central part of Warby Parker's brand story. By showcasing the impact of its donations through photos and stories of the people whose lives have been changed by the gift of sight, Warby Parker creates an emotional connection with its customers. It transforms the act of buying glasses from a mere transaction to a statement of values and a way to make a positive impact on the world.

Warby Parker's story is also one of customer empowerment. The company's Home Try-On program allows customers to select up to five frames to try on at home for free, taking the guesswork and pressure out of the buying process. This program has become a key differentiator for Warby Parker, as it allows customers to experience the brand's products in the comfort of their own homes and on their own terms.

Through its innovative business model, commitment to social responsibility, and focus on customer experience, Warby Parker has crafted a powerful story that resonates with its audience. It is a story of a company that is not just selling glasses, but a lifestyle and a set of values. By aligning itself with the aspirations and ideals of its customers, Warby Parker has built a loyal following and a brand that stands for something greater than just profit.

In conclusion, both Apple's 1984 advertisement and Warby Parker's brand story demonstrate the power of storytelling in business. By tapping into the emotions and aspirations of their audiences, these companies have created narratives that transcend their products and services and establish them as icons of their respective industries. It is through the art of storytelling that businesses can create meaningful connections with their customers and build brands that endure.

* * *

27

The Principle of Anticipating Trends

In the fast-paced, ever-evolving world of business, the ability to anticipate and adapt to emerging trends is not just a valuable skill—it's a necessity. Companies that can successfully navigate the shifting tides of consumer preferences, technological advancements, and market dynamics are the ones that will thrive in the long run. This is where the Principle of Anticipating Trends comes into play.

At its core, the Principle of Anticipating Trends is about developing a keen sense of awareness and foresight. It's about being able to see beyond the horizon, to identify the subtle shifts and changes that will shape the future of your industry. It's about being proactive rather than reactive, and positioning your company to capitalize on emerging opportunities before your competitors even realize they exist.

One of the key principles of anticipating trends is to always keep your finger on the pulse of your industry. This means staying up-to-date with the latest news, research, and insights, and regularly engaging with customers, partners, and other stakeholders to gather feedback and ideas. It also means being open to new perspectives and ways of thinking, and being willing to challenge your own assumptions and biases.

Another important aspect of anticipating trends is to look beyond your own industry and consider the broader context in which your business operates. This means paying attention to demographic shifts, social and cultural changes, and geopolitical events that could impact your business in the future. It also means being aware of emerging technologies and how they could disrupt your industry or create new opportunities for growth.

One company that has mastered the art of anticipating trends is Netflix. From its early days as a DVD-by-mail service to its current status as a global streaming giant, Netflix has consistently been ahead of the curve in terms of understanding and shaping consumer preferences. When the company first launched in 1997, the idea of renting movies online was a novel concept. But Netflix's founders, Reed Hastings and Marc Randolph, saw the potential for a new model of video rental that would be more convenient and affordable than traditional brick-and-mortar stores.

As the internet and streaming technology evolved, Netflix was quick to adapt. The company began offering streaming services in 2007, at a time when many people were still skeptical about the viability of online video. But Netflix had anticipated the shift towards on-demand, personalized content consumption, and had invested heavily in building out its streaming infrastructure and content library.

Today, Netflix is a prime example of a company that has successfully anticipated and capitalized on multiple trends. From the rise of binge-watching and original content production to the growing demand for localized content in international markets, Netflix has consistently been at the forefront of the streaming revolution.

Another company that has demonstrated a keen ability to anticipate trends is Apple. Under the leadership of Steve Jobs, Apple consistently set the standard for innovation and design in the tech industry. Jobs had an uncanny ability to anticipate consumer needs and desires before they even knew what they wanted. He famously said, "People don't know what they want until you show it to them."

This philosophy was evident in the development of products like the iPod, iPhone, and iPad, which revolutionized the way people consumed and interacted with digital content. By anticipating the growing demand for mobile computing and creating devices that were both functional and aesthetically pleasing, Apple was able to capture a significant share of the market and build a fiercely loyal customer base.

But anticipating trends is not just about being first to market with a new product or service. It's also about being able to adapt and pivot when necessary. The COVID-19 pandemic, for example, has forced many companies to rethink their business models and strategies in order to survive. Those that were able to quickly shift to remote work, e-commerce, and digital service delivery were the ones that weathered the storm most effectively.

Companies like Zoom and Peloton saw tremendous growth during the pandemic as people sought out ways to stay connected and active while stuck at home. These companies were able to anticipate the growing demand for remote work and fitness solutions and quickly scale up their operations to meet the needs of their customers.

Of course, anticipating trends is not an exact science. There will always be some level of uncertainty and risk involved. But by developing a culture of curiosity, experimentation, and adaptability, companies can increase their chances of success in an ever-changing business landscape.

One way to cultivate a culture of anticipation is to encourage employees to think like futurists. This means providing opportunities for them to explore new ideas, technologies, and business models, and encouraging them to share their insights and perspectives with others. It also means creating a safe space for experimentation and risk-taking, and recognizing and rewarding those who are willing to challenge the status quo.

Another key aspect of anticipating trends is to be data-driven in your decision-making. By collecting and analyzing data on customer behavior, market trends, and competitor activities, companies can gain valuable insights into emerging opportunities and potential disruptions. This data can also help inform strategic planning and resource allocation, ensuring that companies are investing in the right areas to drive growth and innovation.

However, it's important to recognize that data alone is not enough. Companies must also be able to interpret and act on that data in a timely and effective manner. This requires a combination of analytical skills, business acumen, and creative problem-solving. It also requires a willingness to take calculated risks and make bold decisions when necessary.

Ultimately, the Principle of Anticipating Trends is about developing a mindset of continuous learning and adaptation. It's about being open to new ideas and perspectives, and being willing to let go of old ways of thinking and doing things. It's about being proactive rather than reactive, and always staying one step ahead of the game.

* * *

28

The Principle of Winning Attitude

In business strategy, there is an often-overlooked factor that can make the difference between success and failure: attitude. A winning attitude is not just a feel-good platitude; it is a critical component of any successful business strategy. It is the foundation upon which all other elements of strategy are built, the driving force that propels companies through the inevitable challenges and setbacks that come with the territory.

One company that exemplifies the power of a winning attitude is Nike. Founded by Phil Knight, Nike's success can be attributed in large part to the winning attitudes of its early leadership team. Despite being a group of misfits and castoffs from other companies, Knight's team was united by a common desire to win and a willingness to do whatever it took to achieve success.

Phil Knight's original leadership team consisted of four significant individuals who were all passionate about their work and motivated by challenges rather than money. Jeff Johnson, Knight's first employee, was a runner who couldn't fit into a regular 9-5 job. He had faced personal and professional setbacks, including a divorce, job loss, and a critical accident, before joining Nike. Despite these challenges, Johnson possessed a winning attitude that allowed him to excel in various roles at Nike, from sales to shoe design to factory management, even though he had no prior experience in these areas.

Similarly, Bill Woodall, Nike's operational manager, was a track athlete who had lost his legs in an accident and struggled to find employment. However, his determination and winning attitude transformed Nike's operational management. Del Hayes, the company's accountant, saw accounting as an art form and was passionate about numbers, despite being passed over for a partnership at his previous firm due to his physical appearance and demeanor. Rob Strausser, Nike's lawyer, loved negotiation but hated the insurance industry he came from and couldn't fit into his previous company's policies.

What united these individuals was a shared passion for winning and a willingness to take on any challenge. Phil Knight himself had dreamed of becoming a baseball player but failed to make the college team. He channeled his disappointment into building a company that embodied the spirit of winning. Knight writes that one thing was common among everyone in his leadership team—they had never faced a 'winning' moment in their lives until they joined Nike. Nike was about winning, and each person was willing to do whatever was necessary to win, even if most of the required activities fell outside their area of expertise.

This winning attitude permeated every level of the organization, from the executive suite to the factory floor, and it helped propel Nike to become one of the most iconic and successful brands in the world. It is a testament to the power of cultivating a mindset of resilience, determination, and positivity in the face of challenges and setbacks.

At its core, a winning attitude is a mindset that embraces challenge, seeks out opportunity, and refuses to be deterred by obstacles. It is a way of thinking that views problems as puzzles to be solved rather than roadblocks to be avoided. It is an unwavering belief in the power of hard work, determination, and resilience to overcome even the most daunting of odds.

Cultivating a winning attitude begins with leadership. The tone set by those at the top of an organization has a profound impact on the attitudes and behaviors of those further down the ladder. Leaders who exude positivity, confidence, and a can-do spirit inspire their teams to adopt the same mindset. They lead by example, demonstrating through their actions and decisions that no challenge is too great, no goal too ambitious.

But a winning attitude is not just the province of leadership. It must permeate every level of an organization, from the C-suite to the front lines. This is where culture comes into play. A company culture that values perseverance, creativity, and a willingness to take calculated risks is one that fosters a winning attitude. It is a culture that celebrates successes, learns from failures, and always keeps its eye on the prize.

Another company that embodies the Principle of Winning Attitude is Amazon. From its humble beginnings as an online bookseller to its current status as a global e-commerce giant, Amazon has always been driven by a relentless focus on customer satisfaction and a willingness to think big. Its founder and CEO, Jeff Bezos, is famous for his "Day 1" philosophy, which emphasizes the importance of maintaining a startup mentality no matter how large the company grows.

This winning attitude is reflected in Amazon's culture, which is built around 14 leadership principles that prioritize customer obsession, ownership, and a bias for action. Employees are encouraged to take risks, learn from their mistakes, and always strive to raise the bar. This culture of innovation and continuous improvement has allowed Amazon to disrupt industry after industry, from retail to cloud computing to entertainment.

SpaceX, founded by entrepreneur Elon Musk, is another company that demonstrates the power of a winning attitude. SpaceX has set its sights on nothing less than revolutionizing space travel and colonizing Mars, an audacious goal that requires a level of ambition, creativity, and perseverance that few companies possess. The company's culture is built around a willingness to take on seemingly impossible challenges and find ways to overcome them, as evidenced by its successful launch and landing of the Starship prototype in 2020, a key milestone in its quest to send humans to Mars.

Cultivating a winning attitude is not always easy. It requires a willingness to confront fear, embrace discomfort, and push beyond one's limits. It means being willing to take risks, even in the face of uncertainty and potential failure. It means maintaining a laser-like focus on the end goal, even when the path to get there is unclear.

One way to cultivate a winning attitude is through the power of positive self-talk. The stories we tell ourselves about our abilities and limitations have a profound impact on our actions and outcomes. By consciously choosing to reframe negative self-talk into positive affirmations, we can train our minds to embrace challenge and opportunity.

Another key aspect of a winning attitude is resilience. No matter how well-planned or well-executed a business strategy may be, setbacks and failures are inevitable. What sets successful companies apart is their ability to bounce back from these setbacks and use them as opportunities for growth and learning. This requires a shift in mindset, away from a fear of failure and towards a willingness to embrace it as part of the process. It means viewing failures not as endpoints, but as stepping stones on the path to success. It means being willing to iterate, adapt, and pivot in response to changing circumstances and new information.

Ultimately, the Principle of Winning Attitude is about more than just positive thinking or a can-do spirit. It is a fundamental shift in the way we approach challenges and opportunities, both in business and in life. It is a recognition that our attitudes and beliefs have a powerful impact on our actions and outcomes, and that by cultivating a mindset of resilience, determination, and positivity, we can achieve things that others might dismiss as impossible.

In the world of business strategy, a winning attitude is the fuel that drives innovation, the glue that holds teams together, and the catalyst that turns vision into reality. By embedding this principle into the very fabric of their organizations, companies can create a culture of success that endures long after any individual leader or employee has moved on.

Of course, cultivating a winning attitude is not a one-time event. It requires ongoing effort and attention, a willingness to continually push beyond one's comfort zone and strive for excellence. It means being willing to take risks, learn from failures, and always keep pushing forward, even in the face of adversity.

But for those companies that are willing to put in the work, the rewards can be immense. A winning attitude can be the difference between a company that merely survives and one that thrives, between a business that follows the pack and one that leads it. It is the secret ingredient that separates the good from the great, the successful from the truly extraordinary.

Great leaders are passionate about winning and firmly believe in themselves and their teams. They seek out individuals who share their passion and drive, even if they are considered misfits or have faced setbacks in their careers. By bringing together a diverse group of people united by a common goal and a winning attitude, leaders can create a powerful force for change and innovation.

Ultimately, the Principle of Winning Attitude is about more than just business success. It is about the triumph of the human spirit, the power of perseverance, and the belief that anything is possible with the right mindset. It is a reminder that our greatest limitations are often the ones we place on ourselves, and that by embracing challenges and opportunities with a winning attitude, we can achieve more than we ever thought possible.

* * *

29

Putting It All Together - Implementing Your Business Strategy

In this final chapter, we will explore how you can bring all the principles together, create a cohesive strategy, and put it into action. Follow these steps to make the most of the knowledge you have acquired:

1. Start with your vision: Clearly define your company's long-term goals and aspirations.
2. Establish core values: Identify the guiding principles that will shape your company's culture and decision-making.
3. Hire the right people: Build a team with the skills, experience, and values needed to design, plan, and execute your strategy.
4. Assess your current situation: Take a hard look at your business's current state. Analyze your strengths, weaknesses, opportunities, and threats (SWOT). This will help you identify areas where you can apply the principles you've learned. Be thorough in your assessment, involving key stakeholders and gathering data from various sources. Use this information to set realistic goals and prioritize your strategic initiatives.
5. Understand your customers: Conduct market research to identify your target customer segments and their needs, preferences, and behaviors.
6. Develop your value proposition: Determine how your products or

services will solve your customers' problems and create value for them.
7. Identify core competencies: Determine the key strengths and capabilities that will enable you to deliver your value proposition.
8. Differentiate your business: Identify your unique selling points and how you will differentiate yourself from competitors.
9. Identify strategic activities and ensure strategic fit: Determine the crucial activities that are essential to delivering your value proposition and creating a competitive advantage. These strategic activities should be aligned with your core competencies and differentiation strategy. Prioritize the development and execution of these activities, ensuring that they work together seamlessly to support your overall strategy. Analyze the interrelationships and dependencies between your strategic activities. Look for opportunities to create strategic fit, where the performance of one activity enhances the effectiveness of others. Ensure that each activity is reinforcing and complementing the others, creating a cohesive and synergistic system. Regularly evaluate the alignment of your strategic activities with your value proposition and the evolving market landscape to maintain relevance and competitiveness.
10. Make strategic tradeoffs: Decide what you will and won't do to maintain focus and allocation of resources.
11. Keep the big picture in mind: Adopt a holistic, systems thinking approach to ensure all elements of your strategy align with your overall vision and goals, considering how each part affects the others.
12. Pay attention to detail: Develop detailed plans and processes for every aspect of your business strategy, from product design to execution. Think big, but also think small, as success lies in the details.
13. Identify key resources: Determine the critical assets and resources needed to execute your strategy.
14. Select key partners: Identify strategic partnerships that can help you achieve your goals.
15. Plan customer relationships: Define how you will interact with and support your customers.
16. Choose communication channels: Select the most effective channels for

reaching and engaging your target audience.
17. Foster a strong culture: Develop a company culture that aligns with your values and supports your strategy.
18. Manage finances: Create financial projections and plans to ensure the viability and sustainability of your business.
19. Manage your cost structure and revenue streams: Develop a clear understanding of your cost structure and identify opportunities for optimization. Implement the Principle of Cost Structure to ensure that your costs align with your strategic priorities and value creation. Simultaneously, explore diverse revenue streams and pricing strategies that maximize profitability and sustainability.
20. Build a strong brand and customer relationships: Create a memorable brand identity and nurture long-lasting relationships with your customers. Invest in building a strong, consistent brand across all touchpoints. Focus on delivering exceptional customer experiences and fostering loyalty through personalized interactions and value-added services.
21. Embrace rapid prototyping and iteration: Continuously test, learn, and adapt your strategy based on market feedback.
22. Execute with excellence: Break down your strategy into actionable steps, assign responsibilities, set milestones, and monitor progress. Develop detailed implementation plans, allocate resources effectively, and establish clear performance metrics to track your progress. Maintain a big-picture perspective while paying attention to detail, ensuring that the smaller elements are well-executed and aligned with your overarching strategy.
23. Continuously iterate and adapt: Regularly assess your strategy, anticipate trends, and make necessary adjustments to stay ahead of the curve. Encourage a culture of innovation and experimentation within your organization. Be open to feedback from your customers, employees, and partners, and use it to continuously refine your offerings and processes.
24. Tell your story: Craft a compelling narrative that communicates your vision, values, and unique value proposition.

25. Anticipate trends: Stay informed about industry trends and market shifts, and adapt your strategy accordingly.
26. Maintain a winning attitude: Foster a positive, growth-oriented mindset throughout your organization.

By following these steps, you can create a robust and cohesive business strategy that drives long-term success. Remember, implementing your strategy is an ongoing journey that requires dedication, adaptability, and continuous learning.

As you embark on this journey, stay true to your vision and values, foster a culture of excellence and innovation, and always keep your customers at the heart of your decision-making. Embrace challenges as opportunities for growth and learn from both your successes and failures.

Surround yourself with a strong team, cultivate meaningful partnerships, and engage your stakeholders in your mission. Together, you can overcome obstacles, seize opportunities, and create lasting value for your business and the communities you serve.

* * *

About the Author

Shah Mohammed is an accomplished Business Strategy and design-thinking consultant with a passion for innovation and user-centred design. He is the founder of D-Cube Designs, a leading design consultancy based in Chennai, India. With a Master's degree in Design from IIT Kanpur, India, which he obtained in 2004, Shah brings a strong academic background and a wealth of practical experience to his work.

As an Industrial Designer, Shah has played a pivotal role in successfully developing and launching over 300 products across various industries over the past decade. His expertise spans the entire product lifecycle, from conducting in-depth user research to designing intuitive and aesthetically pleasing solutions. Shah's keen understanding of customer needs and his ability to translate them into innovative product designs have earned him a reputation for excellence in the industry.

In addition to his contributions to the field of design, Shah has also established himself as a sought-after Business Strategy consultant. Leveraging his customer-centric approach, he has provided valuable insights and guidance to businesses of all sizes, helping them identify market opportunities, develop effective strategies, and drive growth. His expertise in areas such as branding, emotional branding, creativity techniques, leadership, and building competitive advantages has made him a trusted advisor to CEOs, startup founders, and aspiring entrepreneurs.

Shah is an avid blogger and has been sharing his knowledge and insights through his blog for the past eight years. With over five hundred articles covering a wide range of topics, including Branding lessons, Design Thinking, Business Strategy, and Psychology in Business, his blog has become a valuable resource for professionals seeking practical advice and inspiration.

You can connect with me on:
- https://www.linkedin.com/in/shahmm
- https://twitter.com/shahbaba
- https://shahmm.medium.com
- https://www.d-cubedesigns.com

Also by Shah Mohammed

The Disruptive Innovation Formula: Strategies to Create Disruptive Innovation in Your Business

The purpose of this book is to provide a short guide to the strategies that companies can use to create disruptive innovations and stay ahead of the curve. Drawing on extensive research and real-world examples, we will explore a wide range of topics, from anticipating future trends and observing extreme users to reimagining business models and breaking functional fixedness.

The goal of this book is to inspire and equip you to become a disruptive innovator in your own industry. Whether you are a seasoned executive or a young entrepreneur, the strategies presented here will help you navigate the challenges and opportunities of the 21st-century business landscape.

The 23 Powerful Laws of Brand Naming: How to Create Brand Names That Stand Out, Connect, and Inspire

In a world where brands are fighting for attention, crafting the perfect name can make all the difference. "The 23 Powerful Laws of Brand Naming" is your ultimate guide to creating brand names that not only stand out from the crowd but also forge deep, lasting connections with your target audience.

Branding expert Shah Mohammed takes you on a captivating journey through the art and science of brand naming, revealing the 23 essential laws that will transform your approach to naming forever.

The Positioning Playbook: The Winning Strategies for Market Dominance

Unlock the secrets to market supremacy with "The Positioning Playbook: The Winning Strategies for Market Dominance." This comprehensive guide dives into the art and science of strategic positioning, revealing the proven strategies that will set your business apart from the competition and propel you to the top of your industry.

Discover the power of positioning, going beyond superficial branding and slogans, to create a deep and lasting impact on your target audience. Learn how to carve out a distinct space in consumers' minds, forging emotional connections and delivering unique value that resonates with their needs and desires.

Throughout the book, readers are introduced to thirteen effective positioning strategies, each serving as a pathway to achieving market dominance and sustainable success.

The Timeless Laws of Branding: The Hidden Keys to Crafting Iconic Brands

Are you tired of branding books that offer fleeting trends and generic advice? Look no further than "The Timeless Laws of Branding: The Hidden Keys to Crafting Iconic Brands." This groundbreaking book unlocks the secrets to building powerful, enduring brands that stand the test of time.

The Heart Market: How to Build an Emotional Brand

In today's crowded marketplace, offering quality products or services is no longer enough. Consumers are seeking deeper connections, emotional resonance, and a sense of belonging that goes beyond mere transactions. Brands that tap into their customers' emotional core will truly thrive in the long run.

Enter "The Heart Market: How to Build an Emotional Brand" by Shah Mohammed - a groundbreaking guide that reveals the secrets to forging powerful emotional bonds between brands and their audiences. This book is a must-read for entrepreneurs, marketers, business leaders, and anyone seeking to create a brand that resonates on a profoundly human level.

Boil The Ocean: The Story of World's Amazing Brands

Embark on a captivating journey through the world of iconic brands with "Boil The Ocean: The Story of World's Amazing Brands." This thought-provoking book offers a collection of insightful case studies that delve into the successes, failures, and transformative moments of some of the most renowned brands in history.

CEO ASAP: Insider Tips from TOP CEOs for Climbing the Corporate Ladder

Welcome to the ultimate guide for aspiring leaders and young professionals aiming to ascend the corporate ladder swiftly and confidently. "CEO ASAP" is your blueprint for success, curated from the wisdom and experiences of top CEOs who have paved the way to the corner office.

Workplace Whispers: Debunking Myths and Paradoxes

Workplace Whispers: Debunking Myths and Paradoxes" is a captivating exploration of the hidden narratives that shape our professional lives. Across its pages, "Workplace Whispers" examines a diverse array of myths and paradoxes that permeate modern organizational culture. From the allure of Simon Sinek's "Starting with Why" to the pitfalls of the Growth Mindset Myth, each chapter offers a fresh perspective on familiar concepts, prompting readers to question deeply held beliefs and assumptions.

The Secret Strategies of Marketing: How Brands Use Cognitive Biases to Win Your Wallet

In a world bombarded by marketing messages, understanding the psychology that underpins consumer behaviour is the ultimate game-changer. Whether you're a marketer, entrepreneur, business owner, or an inquisitive consumer, this book unravels the mysteries behind why certain brands resonate deeply while others remain forgettable.

Your Guide to Cognitive Biases: This comprehensive guide explores a treasure trove of cognitive biases, from the well-known to the lesser-explored, offering profound insights into their applications and impact. From the allure of familiarity to the power of scarcity, you'll journey through a spectrum of biases that influence every purchase decision.

Innovation's Hidden Walls: Uncovering Limitations of Jobs To Be Done, Design Thinking, and the Diffusion of Innovation Model

In "Innovation's Hidden Walls," we delve deep into the core principles of Jobs To Be Done (JTBD), Design Thinking, and the Diffusion of Innovation Model. While these methodologies have been celebrated for sparking innovation, this book takes a critical look at their limitations. Discover how these walls can restrict your innovation endeavours, and learn how to break through them to truly transform your approach to problem-solving.

Disrupting Perfection: Uncovering the Limitations of Dieter Rams' Design Principles

"Disrupting Perfection" challenges the conventional wisdom surrounding Dieter Rams' celebrated design principles by delving into their limitations and exploring alternative perspectives on design excellence. This thought-provoking book critiques each of Rams' principles and presents compelling examples that challenge their applicability in contemporary design practice. Through insightful analysis and real-world case studies, readers are invited to reconsider established design norms and embrace a more nuanced understanding of design innovation and user experience.

SUB-BRANDING PLAYBOOK: Winning Strategies for Targeted Growth

In this captivating playbook, you'll discover a treasure trove of sub-branding strategies, each chapter unveiling a different secret weapon to unlock targeted growth. From creating sub-brands for demographic segmentation to psychographic targeting and cultural branding, we leave no stone unturned.

The book provides insights into successful sub-branding initiatives through real-world case studies, offering practical, actionable strategies for leveraging sub-brands to achieve targeted growth. By examining the considerations and criteria for developing sub-brands, readers can understand how sub-brands contribute to brand differentiation, customer targeting, and market expansion.

Elevate your brand's position, attract a loyal customer base, and surpass your competition. The Sub-Branding Playbook is your trusted companion on this exciting adventure, offering guidance, inspiration, and a roadmap to targeted growth.

Breaking Chains: A Manager's Playbook for Becoming a Leader

Embark on a transformative journey from managerial expertise to visionary leadership with "Breaking Chains: A Manager's Playbook for Becoming a Leader." This compelling book redefines leadership, offering invaluable insights and strategies for individuals striving to ascend from managerial roles to impactful leadership positions. Rooted in real-world scenarios and enriched by a wealth of leadership wisdom, this playbook provides a roadmap for professional growth and organizational success.

Unveiling the Managerial Metamorphosis: In the fast-paced landscape of contemporary business, the transition from a manager to a leader is a profound evolution. "Breaking Chains" explores this metamorphosis, unraveling the core shifts that propel individuals from functional mastery to strategic leadership. Drawing inspiration from Michael D. Watkins' HBR article, the playbook delves into transformative factors such as Specialist to Generalist, Analyst to Integrator, Tactician to Strategist, and so on.

www.ingramcontent.com/pod-product-compliance
Lightning Source LLC
Chambersburg PA
CBHW071458220526
45472CB00003B/850